PARENTING
LET'S MAKE A GAME OF IT

---

*Playful ways to stop struggling with your child
and start having more fun*

KAREN THURM SAFRAN

First paperback edition March 2019
Cover design by Mila Milic (www.milagraphicartist.com)
Author photo by Rene Sorensen
ISBN-13: 978-0-578-46163-2
www.ParentingLetsMakeAGameOfIt.com

In loving memory of my parents who were positive, playful, and empowering, and are deeply missed.

With great admiration for my children, who continue to make me incredibly proud to be their mom.

For my boyfriend and partner, Andrew, whose love, support, and encouragement made this book a reality.

CONTENTS

INTRODUCTION

When I started first grade, my dad had a clever idea of walking me to school each morning. What a perfect solution! He could get his daily exercise while also spending quality time with his youngest child.

Or so he thought.

But instead of this being a positive experience, every day I dragged my feet and complained. "Again? Can't we drive like everyone else?" It was not fun for either one of us.

Most parents would have given up, but not my dad.

Then one morning something changed.

Before I could start fussing, my dad bounced into the room like Tigger, took my hand, and twirled me out the front door singing in a silly voice, "Get ready to play the Name-It game! Do you know? Do you know? What's the capital of Idaho?" With a wink, he lifted me higher as I skipped along, eagerly waiting for the answer. "Think potatoes. Boise potatoes. Boise is the capital of Idaho!"

That day, our morning ritual was transformed, and walking became an enchanting experience.

By the time I graduated from elementary school, not only had we walked nearly one thousand miles together, but I also had learned all fifty state capitals, many world capitals, and other facts. More importantly, my dad and I shared countless special moments during those early morning hours.

When I became a mom, I experienced firsthand the benefits of this positive, playful approach. It made parenting more fun, empowered my kids, and provided quality family time.

Let's face it, being a parent is incredibly rewarding, but it's also stressful. There are ongoing power struggles and never-ending issues. It's a lot of hard work!

Trust me, as a stressed-out single parent, I was far from relaxed. And being divorced with two young children made it especially difficult since I could no longer depend on another adult in the house to help out. Nope, I was on my own, so it was even more crucial to solving challenging situations creatively. Throughout the years, I also learned the importance of being mindful, breathing deeply, and not giving up on ideas—even when I was exhausted and ready to scream.

I'm neither a therapist nor a child expert. I'm a mom with two grown kids and have spent my entire life immersed in this playful technique. If this strategy helped me, it can help anyone. While this book is loosely based on how I raised my kids, the people, events, and details are fictitious.

Parenting—Let's Make a Game of It is not your typical self-help book. The "how to" lessons are told through quick to read, light-hearted stories to spark your playfulness, encourage out-of-the-box thinking, and ease frustrating moments. The stories stand alone, so you can read them sequentially or in any order, based on a particular parenting challenge. This book is helpful for parents, grandparents, and anyone who works with children.

I encourage you to visit bit.ly/ParentingExtras where you can download several free resources. This includes the charts, calendars, and images from this book, as well as other goodies to help you become a more playful, positive parent.

Like most parents, the mom in this book, Carrie, faces everyday frustrations during her children's preschool through elementary school years. Her kids, Emily and Justin, are impatient, not listening, uncooperative, upset, and even having meltdowns. When Carrie changes her approach, things quickly improve. Soon her kids willingly listen. Tension turns to quality time. And life becomes more playful.

Regardless of the children's ages in each story, you can adapt the playfulness to nearly any age. Surprisingly, I still incorporate many in my life today. And my kids are grown and living on their own!

After reading a few stories or the entire book, you might start seeing things in new ways. Don't be surprised if soon you're entertained while waiting in lines, experience museums playfully, dance on turbulent flights, and approach life with a more joyful attitude.

So, what are you waiting for? Parenting, let's make a game of it!

Part I

Ugh, My Child Won't Cooperate

1

PUMPKIN, PUMPKIN, DRINK

Getting Kids to Drink When They're Sick

"NO! No drink!" Emily shouts, pounding the kitchen table to emphasize her two-year-old powers. After peering at me with a deep, piercing glare, she resumes coloring her pumpkin drawing. A moment later and for the umpteenth time this morning, my daughter opens her mouth, scrunches her nose, and propels her head forward. "Achoo!"

"God bless you. As I was saying, you need to drink when you're sick because—"

"NO! Me no drink."

I cringe and shake my head. *Welcome to the Terrible Twos.*

It's October, the beginning of cold and flu season, and Emily's sneezing is getting worse. She must drink fluids. I have to do something, so I stride to the refrigerator to get her favorite beverage. On my way, I slide Justin and his activity mat farther away from his sister and her sneezing germs. Yeah, the odds are high that my newborn son will also get sick, but at least I can try to delay it.

"Yummy, I'm getting coconut water. Do you want some?" I ask, waving the container.

3

This time, Emily doesn't even bother to look up. Instead, she leans closer to her drawing and scribbles broad, orange strokes. "NO! Me fine."

While my jaw clenches tighter, I reassure myself. *My daughter isn't stubborn. She's strong-willed. And this is a positive trait.*

"Achoo!"

With this next sneeze, Emily wipes her nose on the closest item, her sleeve.

Yuck.

Hastily, I put back the coconut water, grab a few tissues, and dash over. "Here, sweetie, in case you get tired of your runny nose."

"Mommy silly. Nose no run." She giggles.

"You're a silly willy," I say, cleaning her dripping nose and kissing her head. Then I try again, this time offering a choice. "Would you like apple juice or water?"

No response.

Now what? She needs to drink, and I refuse to give in to a two-year-old's power.

Think, Carrie, think. I must outsmart her. What can I do?

Sighing, I glance around in search of some inspiration and see piles of mail, unwashed dishes, crayons, her drawing—

Yes, a bright orange pumpkin!

It's the Halloween season with pumpkins on every porch. And now I have an idea. Even though I'm excited to implement my plan, I approach my daughter cautiously.

"Wow, you're doing a nice job coloring."

Big smile.

"Have you ever played the game Pumpkin, Pumpkin, Drink?"

Hearing the words "game" and "pumpkin," Emily squeals and flutters her hands. "Ooh, me play!"

"And we get to go outside. It's not cold, but you'll need a sweater."

Emily tosses the orange crayon across the table and reaches up high, wiggling her fingers. "Uppie, uppie!"

In one full motion, I unbuckle her booster seat and hoist her out of the kitchen chair. As soon as her purple sneakers touch the ground, she runs to the row of jackets and sweaters hanging on hooks.

Not surprisingly, she sneezes again. "Achoo!"

Seconds later, Emily darts back to the kitchen carrying her favorite sweater and Justin's sweatshirt. "Me blue. Baby Justin green."

"You're so helpful. Thank you." With one hand to keep her steady, I slip the sweater over her fidgeting body. Then I lift my cheerful son from his mat and put the sweatshirt on him. "You are so lucky to have Emily as your big sister," I say, tickling his tummy.

Emily skips in circles chanting, "Baby Justin, Baby Justin," which makes him coo even louder.

Once my little cheerleader simmers down, I place Justin in his stroller, slip on my coat, and open the door. "Are you ready to play Pumpkin, Pumpkin, Drink?"

"Whee!" Emily exclaims. She extends her arms and flies out the door like an airplane, leading our little entourage.

Now comes the good part!

Pausing, I silently count to three. "Emily, one moment. I forgot the most important thing. Drinks for our game. Silly me."

"Mommy silly." She giggles.

5

"What color water bottle do you want? Blue or green?" I tightly cross my fingers behind my back and wait. *Hope my plan works.*

"Green! Green!"

"Great choice. Wait here and I'll be back in a second." Right away, I run inside the house and grab the drinks, which, of course, were already prepared in the fridge. "Here you go," I say, placing the green water bottle in her outstretched hand.

By now, I'm feeling quite confident, but I'm still antsy since we haven't started the game. Holding my head high, I wave her drawing. "Let's walk around the neighborhood and find your favorite thing— pumpkins!"

"Pumpkins!" Emily squeals, followed by another sneeze.

"Every time we see one, we'll sing 'Pumpkin, pumpkin, drink,' and then we drink. Look! There's a pumpkin by our door." With a big smile, I raise my bottle high, like it's a trophy, before gulping the water.

"Yay! Pumpkin, pumpkin, drink," she says and takes several mouthfuls.

Wow, this is easier than I thought.

"Again!" Emily grabs my hand and drags us next door. As expected, when she sees the neighbor's pumpkins, she jumps up and down and immediately belts out, "Pumpkin, pumpkin, drink."

I wait for her to finish slurping her water before pointing to the porch. "Ooh, there's also a little pumpkin by the big one. You know what that means."

This time, Emily dances around the stroller and waves her bottle in front of Justin, who kicks his legs and coos like he's singing with us. For the next ten minutes, we continue playing, stopping at each house to sing, squeal, and drink.

Well, what do you know! There are pumpkins everywhere.

Yup, it's the Halloween season, so there's at least one pumpkin on every porch and sometimes a whole group of them. After we stroll down our block and turn the corner, Emily unexpectedly starts crying.

Uh-oh. So much for my plan.

Her crying intensifies and she stomps the ground, tipping her water bottle upside down. "More!"

"Emily, it's okay," I say, exhaling with relief. "Look what I have in here."

Right away, she scurries over and pokes her head inside the bag attached to the stroller. Since I'm just as quick, I wipe her dripping nose before taking out the surprise. "Yay! Your blue water bottle. We can keep playing."

"Mommy!" Emily cheers and wraps her arms around my legs for a quick hug, careful not to spill her drink.

"Hey, I have an idea. Do you and Justin want to dress up as pumpkins for Halloween?"

"Pummmm-pkiiiiiiiiins!" Without waiting, Emily runs toward the next house with its cluster of pumpkins. Before we can catch up, her sweet singing resonates along the sidewalk.

"Well, Justin"—I ruffle his hair and wink—"being strong-willed is definitely a wonderful trait. Here's to pumpkins and Halloween, my new favorite holiday."

2

PROUD MEMBER OF THE CLEAN PLATE CLUB

Eating with Manners

I feel like shouting "Justin, stop!" Instead, I cringe silently, watching my four-year-old son lift his tomato-smeared plate, open his mouth, and stick out his tongue.

Surely, he'll stop.

But he doesn't. His six-year-old sister, Emily, watches and giggles.

Are you kidding? No way!

"Aw, pisghetti," Justin exclaims, smacking his lips as if in a post-eating, dreamy trance. His tongue darts around the plate, slurping and lapping up the leftover sauce.

"Young man! What are you doing?" I bang my fist on our kitchen table so hard that the silverware rattles.

And just like that, he snaps out of his hypnotic state and pokes his head from behind the plate. "But Mommy, it's yummy."

Before I can say anything else, Justin quickly runs his tongue over his lips, savoring whatever's left of his favorite meal.

"Is that how you'd eat in a restaurant?" My eyes lock with his, and I'm so flabbergasted that it's hard to speak.

He shrugs and lowers his plate back on the table.

"I'm glad you love the spaghetti dinner, but that's *not* how we eat."

"I don't wanna leave any. It's so good."

Emily flashes Justin her big-sister protective smile and looks at me. As she clears her throat, she sits up straight like someone about to make an important announcement. "Mommy, he's a member of the Clean Plate Club."

Now this situation has become somewhat comical.

Yeah, real funny when he licks his plate clean at a friend's house. Yikes, or years later with a date! What should I do? While I struggle with my internal dialogue, my kids fidget and stare, waiting for my reaction.

Then it hits me.

Yes! I'll use his inappropriate behavior to encourage proper table manners. No reason to stop licking your plate clean when you can go all-out eating like a puppy dog. Hey, I'm not the only parent to teach a lesson through reverse psychology.

"Wow, you're eating like a puppy, licking up every last bit," I say, wiping my squirming son's mouth.

"Yeah." And to prove my point, Justin leaps off his chair and jumps around on all fours. "I'm a puppy! I'm a puppy!"

With a plan in place and a smirk, I whisper the unthinkable. "Do you want to eat like a puppy dog?"

"Ruff ruff!" His head flutters up and down while he begs with curved hands.

Emily flips her head back and forth between Justin and me. Should she look at her brother who is acting like a dog? Or at me, since I seem to have lost my mind?

"If you eat nicely this week, you can eat like a puppy at dinner on Saturday."

"M-m-mommy?" Emily blinks. This news leaves her completely baffled, so I wink to signal that everything is under control.

To continue with my plan, I turn back to Justin. "What should you do to eat like a puppy for your special Saturday dinner treat?"

He throws his head back and howls like a euphoric dog. "Eat nicely-y-y-y! Ruff!"

Realizing that I am serious, Emily says to Justin with her grown-up voice, "That's Tuesday, Wednesday, Thursday, *and* Friday."

"Ruff!" Justin slides off the chair and brings his plate to the sink. Then, bright-eyed, he darts back and gives me a big kiss—puppy style.

Emily skips over and hugs the non-slobbery side of my face, whispering, "Mommy, this is gonna be fun."

"And funny," I add.

For the rest of the week, Justin has impeccable manners. Shockingly so, like he's attending an etiquette dining class, using his utensils properly, and saying "please" and "thank you."

Each night I give positive encouragement, "Way to go!" and he responds with a "Ruff!" wagging his imaginary tail. And at the end of every meal, Emily counts on her fingers the remaining number of days.

At long last, the big event arrives: Saturday dinner.

"Are you ready? It's dinner time," I say extra loud, so they can hear me from down the hall.

Within moments, I hear the pitter-patter of feet and see Justin prancing around the corner on all fours, joyfully barking. Emily follows, clasping her purple sparkly belt, fastened to his pants like a leash. "Meet our cute new puppy!"

This is funnier than I imagined.

"Look where you get to eat!" I exclaim, pointing to the ground where several placemats are carefully arranged to protect the floor. And in the middle, Justin discovers a plate with his favorite meal: pisghetti. Tonight it looks especially delicious with lots of tomato sauce oozing over the long strands of pasta.

"Ruff ruff!"

Emily peers down at his food and then at me. "Mommy, really?"

"It's okay," I say, which relaxes her shoulders. She ruffles Justin's hair, drops the leash, and climbs on her chair.

During the next few minutes, we observe Justin on all fours, tackling his spaghetti without any utensils. He takes a large bite, but globs of noodles hang from his mouth, making it difficult to swallow.

It doesn't take long for him to ask, "Hey, where's my fork?"

"Silly puppy. Doggies don't eat with a fork." I shake my head and try not to chuckle.

Emily's grin widens. "Silly puppy."

"Ruff!" Justin wiggles his butt and drops his head into the mound of spaghetti. This time, he tries sucking a strand which gradually enters his mouth.

Throughout dinner, Emily and I savor our meal while keeping an eye on Justin.

After struggling more with his dinner, Justin lifts his head. Yeeks! His face is covered with sauce, and pieces of spaghetti dangle from both cheeks.

"Ruff," he says, but this time with less enthusiasm. I bite my lip hard to stifle my laughter.

11

Minutes later, Justin looks up again and sighs. "Mommy, this is really hard. And pisghetti is my favorite. Can I have a fork? Please?"

Phew, my plan hasn't backfired.

"But you wanted to eat like a puppy. Aren't you having fun?" I ask.

"Not really," he quietly mumbles with an unenergetic "ruff."

"Is doggie Justin ready to be big boy Justin and eat nicely at the table?"

"Ruff. I mean, yeah."

At once, Emily runs to the kitchen cabinet, takes a fork from the drawer, and hands it to her brother who is now sitting nicely on his chair. "Here ya go, our big boy."

Meanwhile, I clean Justin's messy face with a cloth I had tucked under my plate. "I guess eating like a puppy dog isn't as much fun as you thought?"

"Nope," he mutters. Without waiting any longer, Justin smiles, grasps his fork, and then digs into his beloved meal. "Aw, pisghetti!"

POSTSCRIPT

I recently shared this story with my grown son who enlightened me. "Hey, Mom, remember when I always got up to clear my dish? You thought I was such a well-behaved kid. Well actually, at the sink with no one looking, I would triumphantly lick my plate clean, every last bit." Then he hugged me and whispered, "Ruff!"

3

DO WE HAVE TO VISIT A DUMB ART MUSEUM?

Making Museum Visits Fun

"I don't wanna go to some dumb art museum!" My five-year-old son, Justin, stomps across the hotel room and throws himself on the bed, which makes the headboard smack loudly against the wall. Great, as if his shouting isn't creating enough of a disturbance.

Here's to a fun Washington DC visit with my kids.

I rub my pesky, twitching eye and march over to him. "This museum is one of the best. Get up!"

Justin raises his head just long enough to glare at me.

Seven-year-old Emily sashays to the bed and sits near her younger brother. "Don't you know?" she says. "He doesn't like *any* art museum."

Even though I'm seething inside, I exhale slowly to the count of three. Yelling won't accomplish anything, so I push aside my frustration and try another approach. "Oh, I have something exciting to share. Guess what else is in DC? A museum with dinosaurs!"

"Di-no-saurs?" Justin lifts his face, smiling.

"Yup, and a zoo with a giant panda," I say, enticing him with other favorite kid-friendly spots.

"I love zoos!" He leaps off the bed while Emily jumps up and clasps her hands.

"Ooh, a giant panda. How cute."

"If we leave now, I can take you to the zoo after lunch. First, we'll go to a museum, the—"

"Dinosaurs and zoo," Justin interrupts.

"No, the *art museum* and zoo," I say without blinking.

As expected, they groan.

After a few moments of silence, Emily speaks very slowly and deliberately, which puts me on high alert that she's up to something. "Let's vote to decide."

"That's not fair. Two against one," I say, talking faster to regain control of the situation. "We'll play Rock-Paper-Scissors to decide. One time. The winner gets to choose which museum we'll go to today. Tomorrow, we'll visit the museum that didn't win. And *no* complaining. None! Got it?"

I stare until they nod.

Emily looks at Justin and announces, "I'll play for us." Without waiting for his approval, she flexes her hand. "One, two, three."

"Rock-Paper-Scissors!" the three of us shout. While I show two fingers, Emily flashes her five pink nails.

"Scissors cuts paper, so I win," I say. "Don't worry. We'll have fun at the art museum, and tomorrow we'll see dinosaurs. Remember, no complaining." Grabbing our things, I escort my sulking kids out the door.

Fortunately, the Metro train ride is quick, and after a short walk, we climb the steep steps of the National Gallery of Art.

Justin looks around the massive lobby, and his shoulders droop.

"Oh no, this place is gi-gan-tic," Emily grumbles. Then hastily she adds, "Just so you know, I wasn't complaining. That was a fact."

"I promise, we'll only be here for one hour."

Emily glances at her watch, takes a museum guide from the counter, and thrusts it in my face.

Because she's timing me, I grab their hands and swiftly maneuver us through the halls to the first room. My heart races with fond memories of entertaining art museum visits with my mom and aunt. Now it's my turn to carry the tradition to the next generation.

"Get ready to play Grandma and Aunt Victoria's museum games! Close your eyes. When I count to three, find the *Little Dancer*. I'll give you a clue. She's not a painting. She's a sculpture."

At once, I start counting. On three, their eyes pop open and glance around while I keep talking. "Look for a ballerina in a plastic box. She's wearing—"

"Over there!" Justin points and darts over to the *Little Dancer*.

By this point, my adrenaline has skyrocketed. "Check this out," I say. "The artist, Degas, wanted the statue to look like an actual dancer. So what did he do? He dressed her in a fabric tutu, linen ballet slippers, and a silk hair ribbon, just like the actual fourteen-year-old dancer wore."

I stop talking and stretch my hands behind my back to imitate her stance. "Look, I'm standing like his model." After holding this position, I loosen my arms and place them around my kids. "If you were the artist, how would you want the model to stand?"

With a big smile, Emily lifts her hands above her head. Justin puffs out his chest and swings out one leg, wobbling to keep his balance.

"Nice, except for one thing. The model has to hold still for a long time. Could you stay like that for hours?"

Emily giggles as Justin sways and topples over.

Aware of my time commitment, I take their hands and lead us to a large painting with several dancers. "This is called *Four Dancers*, also by Degas. Look at it. Does it seem like the dancers are standing still or moving?"

Emily tilts her head and squints. "Moving?"

"Yes. See the ballerinas' arms? They're pointed in different directions like we're watching them stretch." Even though my kids are young, I can't help explaining more about one of my favorite artists. "Degas is known for using angles to create a sense of movement. He wanted people to see that dancers are always moving, even when they're waiting."

"Hey, let's pretend we're in this painting," Justin says. He leans over with a bent arm, and Emily slides next to him, raising one hand.

"Mommy, you too," she says. "Then there will be seven, not four, dancers!"

Are these my kids? They're really getting into this museum visit.

We untangle ourselves and enter the attached room. "These cathedral paintings are by the artist Monet, who was part of the Impressionist movement. That's when artists painted outside in order to show how light can change the way things look. Do you think these paintings are of the same or different cathedrals?"

Justin hesitates and studies the paintings. "Different?"

Emily chuckles. "The same or you wouldn't ask."

"They look different because of their colors, but it's actually the same cathedral painted at various times. Like when it was sunny and cloudy. During sunrise and sunset. And other times throughout the day when the light changed."

"They're so pretty," Emily says, gazing at each one.

Gently, I push my kids near one of the paintings. "Close up, it's blotches of color that don't look like anything. Now step back and watch the cathedral magically appear."

"Oh, let's count our steps," Justin says, slowly walking backward. "Six! Six steps to see the cathedral."

We're having so much fun that I want to stay longer, but it's almost lunchtime and we should go. As a friend always tells me, stop while you're having fun. Besides, Emily will soon remind me of my one-hour limit.

"Anyone hungry?" I ask. "Let's get food and then head to the zoo."

Justin furrows his eyebrows and sighs. "Already? Do we really have to go?"

POSTSCRIPT

I was looking at photos of my twenty-two-year-old son's recent visit to London and Amsterdam with his girlfriend. As I flipped through the photos, I couldn't help chuckling when I saw several pictures of them inside museums, standing in silly poses next to paintings and sculptures. *Well, look at that!*

4

SIXTY PACKETS OF OATMEAL

Using a Bar Graph to Incentivize Kids

Without warning, a deluge of oatmeal boxes and loose packets tumble from the top kitchen cabinet. Luckily the packets are soft, otherwise, I'd have black and blue marks on my head.

So here I stand, half asleep, surrounded by dozens of instant oatmeal packages. "Breakfast, anyone?"

Justin, who's five, twists his body in the seat to see the commotion. "I'll have waffles."

Waffles! Really?

Emily slides off her chair and comes to my rescue, plopping amidst the large pile.

"Can you believe all this oatmeal?" I say.

"How come we have so many packets?" Justin asks. Thankfully, he's now focused on oatmeal and forgets his waffle request.

"That's a good question." Usually, I have a rough idea of the food inventory, but, obviously, I've been slacking off on my oatmeal tallying.

"We *love* oatmeal," Emily exclaims. "Whenever we shop, I always throw a box into the cart."

"I do too," admits Justin with a guilty smile.

"And sometimes I do the same thing. But this is way too much for our small cabinet."

"We have so-o-o much," Justin says.

"Gee, I wonder how many?" I mumble half to myself, half aloud. "There are four unopened boxes, two empty boxes, and lots of packets spread all over the floor. Each box holds twelve packets. Yikes! That means we have around sixty—"

"Sixty!" Justin drops his head into his hand.

"Sixty!" Emily shouts. "That's so funny. We could open an oatmeal store."

This is way too much. And it will be challenging shoving the packets back into the cabinet without another oatmeal explosion.

My brain revs into calculation mode. "Let's see, if we each eat one every morning, that will be three a day. Which means it will take about twenty days or three weeks to use them up."

I glance at my kids. "And that's if we eat one a day."

Like that will ever happen.

To confirm my thought, Justin looks up. "Hey, what about waffles? We don't want oatmeal every morning."

"Yeah." Emily glares at me.

Think, Carrie, think. How can I get them to switch back to oatmeal?

Sure, most people wouldn't care nor waste a moment thinking about this ridiculous problem. But I'm not normal.

"Wa-ffles, wa-ffles, wa-ffles," Emily says, encouraging Justin to join in.

Lovely. My union leader has started an oatmeal strike.

"Wa-ffles, wa-ffles, wa-ffles," they chant.

Desperately, I look around the kitchen and adjoining room in search of an idea. Sink, dishes, photos, pens, books, board games—

Games, that's it.

We love challenges, so I'll create a game for eating oatmeal.

With a purpose and plan in place, I grab a piece of paper, a pen, and colored pencils. Not wasting any time, I draw two lines.

Right away, the chanting stops and two heads huddle over my scribbling hand. Next to the horizontal line, I write our names.

"That's us." Emily points and explains in her big-sister voice, "Here's you, Justin."

"I know! I can read my name."

By the tall vertical line, I write "Oatmeal Packets" and jot down numbers one through thirty. With three people eating oatmeal, I figure this should be high enough.

"What are you doing?" Justin scoots closer.

"I'm creating a graph."

"Ooh!" Emily says. "My teacher made one to show the number of pets we all have."

"Yup, graphs show info in a way that's quick and easy to read. Like we're going to do with our Oatmeal Eating game."

Justin's eyes pop open, and he collapses into giggles. "An Oatmeal Eating game? That's so silly."

Still entranced with her classroom graph, Emily rambles on. "We have dogs, cats, hamsters, and birds. Someone even has a rabbit. Dogs won. *Twenty* dogs!"

"Imagine that, twenty dogs," I say, and then steer us back to the matter at hand: oatmeal.

"There are different types of graphs. This one is a bar graph. See this high line? It's the number of oatmeal packets. As you know, this bottom line has our names. Now, here comes the fun part."

Justin perks up.

"When someone eats a packet of oatmeal, that person will color one row above their name."

Eyeing the colored pencils next to us, Emily blurts out, "I'm purple—"

"Yellow! I'm yellow," Justin shouts.

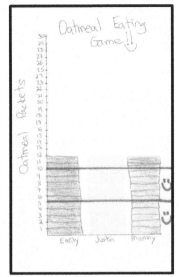

"Okay, I'll be blue. As I was saying, when you eat oatmeal packets, your bar grows taller. This graph will show how much oatmeal you've eaten."

"Um, what's the game?" Justin peers at me, scowling.

"Aha! The goal is to eat oatmeal for breakfast. The more you eat, the taller your bar gets, and ta-da, the more oatmeal we'll use up."

Some reaction, but not enough. I better add something else.

"Also, there will be prizes at different levels."

"Prizes!" Justin cheers.

"Now we're talking," Emily says, and then her animated eyes squint with skepticism. "What kind of prizes?"

Right.

As two kids eagerly stare, I think of a spur-of-the-moment reward system. "After we each eat five packets, we'll eat out. And we'll see a movie when we use up *all* the oatmeal."

Emily smiles smugly. "Then we'll go to the store and buy *more* oatmeal."

Justin shakes his head, snickering. "And then we'll have to draw another graph and start all over again."

"You two are funny, and I love you." I pull us into a tight embrace. "Now, what do you want for breakfast?"

Emily glances at her brother with mischievous eyes, and Justin returns the devilish smirk. Together they shout, "Waffles!" as they sort through the pile of oatmeal packets to choose their favorite flavor.

5

A PLAYFUL LET'S-KEEP-THE-HOUSE-NEAT UNPACKING GAME

Using Music to Make Chores Fun

Uh-oh. What's that noise?

It came from the living room and sounded like items falling. Wait, now my kids are giggling. What are they up to? We arrived home from the airport only fifteen minutes ago, and something has already happened?

I peek around the corner and see our backpacks, suitcases, and bags scattered everywhere.

And I mean everywhere.

"That was awesome, but I told you the backpack would topple it over," Emily says, watching her six-year-old brother jump over bags like he's leaping hurdles.

"Mommy, you should have seen my humongous tower of luggage." Justin runs into my arms when he notices me standing there.

"It was really tall." Emily reaches high with a hop and then collapses on the floor.

Wow. Despite the six-hour flight, they sure have lots of energy.

I stare at the bags, and they seem to glare back. A stark reminder that it will take a long time to unpack.

Sure, most people would wait, but we have guests coming tomorrow morning. We could shove our luggage to the side, but that brings me to the second and real reason. I'm a neat freak and like to unpack right away.

"Your tower must have been tall because that's a lot of stuff. Here comes the fun part of our trip —unpacking."

"That's NOT fun," Justin shouts.

"Hel-lo. She's being sarcastic." Emily skips to her room with Justin trailing behind her.

"Hey! Where are you both going? Our friends are visiting, so we have to put everything away."

"To my room. It missed me," Emily says over her shoulder.

"I wanna play with my Legos."

Seriously?

"Come on! We're a family, so we all need to help."

I stride to their rooms with heavy steps, and I don't know which is louder, my yelling or my stomping feet.

Emily looks up from her bed, expressionless. Will she be sweet to win me over? Or firm to push back? Before I can guess, she lifts her arms and crosses them over her chest.

Lovely, she's going with the headstrong option.

"I do not want to unpack," she says, locking eyes with mine. When I don't respond, she immediately softens her approach. "Mommy, this trip was so special. I want to sit in my room and remember it."

Does she really think I'll fall for this?

I motion her to the living room and walk across the hall to get Justin. "You heard me. Let's go. Now!"

His response is silent but powerful: a piercing glare.

Don't explode, Carrie. Breathe and focus on the nice trip.

With a calming breath, I smile, remembering my mom swirling Emily and Justin around the kitchen, dancing as we prepared dinner. That's my mom, a master of playfulness, with music as her trick for making anything fun.

Of course. Music.

"We're going to play a Grandma type of game. Justin, get the two laundry baskets. Emily, get our favorite music—"

"*The Lion King!*"

Ah, how my girl loves anything Disney.

When we meet at the toppled tower of bags, I twirl around with the laundry baskets propped on my head. "We're going to play a Let's-Keep-The-House-Neat Unpacking game."

"No fair, that's NOT a game," Justin shouts.

"Sure it is. It's a race to see how fast we can unpack. Let's guess how many songs it will take. Each song lasts about three min—"

"Four songs!" Emily interrupts.

"Three!" Justin yells.

I hold up my hand and wiggle my fingers. "Five songs. Here's our plan. First, we'll sort everything into the laundry baskets based on where stuff goes in the house. Next, we'll deliver and put away those items. This will minimize racing back and forth."

To keep up the momentum, I start the Disney music. "First song. Go, team, go!"

Racing back, I unzip Emily's suitcase. Everything is organized, so I swiftly transfer her folded clothes into a laundry basket.

Emily's hands sneak around me and removes her shoes. In one motion, she pulls off the shower caps covering the dirty soles and starts two piles. "Bathroom stuff goes here, and this area is for my shoes."

Meanwhile, Justin turns their backpacks upside down. Water bottles, leftover snack food, empty bags, crumpled napkins, travel games, cards, and books tumble out. At once, he starts separating items. "Here's the kitchen pile. Here's one for books and games."

"Wow, you're both so quick. Justin, when you're done, deliver the books and games to the entertainment shelf." I place the rest of Emily's clothes into the laundry basket. "Go, Emily, go!"

Without a moment to spare, she slides the basket down the hall to her room. Right away, I hear drawers opening and closing while she shoves clothes inside.

"Second s-o-o-o-o-ng," Justin announces with a big yawn.

"Sleepy? It's been a long day traveling," I say.

"Nah." Then more energetically, he exclaims, "My suitcase next!"

"Got it. I'll empty your bag, and you deliver the kitchen pile." I point to the mound behind me and rattle off instructions. "Put snacks in the snack bin, water bottles in the sink, and garbage in the trash can." Justin snatches the items, scurries around the kitchen, and soon the pile disappears.

When Emily returns with the empty laundry basket, I'm almost finished sorting his suitcase. Without wasting any time, she grabs the shoes and dashes back to their rooms.

"Justin, throw these dirty clothes in the laundry bins. Remember to separate the darks from the whites," I say.

Grinning, he tosses them in the hampers like a basketball pro, shouting, "Score!" with each dunk.

I set aside his bathroom stuff and zip close his suitcase. "Done! Justin's laundry basket is ready for delivery."

"I-I-I-I-I-I got it," he says with another big yawn, and he drags his feet down the hall, pushing the laundry basket.

"Woo-hoo! Only Mommy's suitcase and bag are left. And we're on the third song." Emily exclaims, grabbing Justin's bathroom items.

Amazing, we're nearly finished.

Moving at lightning speed, Emily and I focus on emptying and sorting my things. After a while, she looks up. "Hey, where's Justin?" She takes my shoes and walks toward our rooms. "Ju-stin, are you almost—Whoa! Mommy, come here. This is so funny."

What's going on? I leave my bag and follow her giggles where I find an empty laundry basket… and Justin, sound asleep on his floor.

Well, the six-hour flight and jet lag finally caught up with him.

"Mommy, he was right about three songs. Not for unpacking, but for falling asleep. It looks like I was also right. We're almost done, so it *will* take four songs to finish. Yay!"

And I was correct too. Our unpacking game worked. The house is neat, ready for our guests, and we had fun doing it. As a bonus, it wore out my hyper son, who is now sleeping.

"So, who won the unpacking race?" Emily asks.

"We all did!" I exclaim. "Now we don't have to bother unpacking tomorrow."

6

OOH, WHERE DO YOU WANT TO GO?

Engaging Kids While Walking to the Airport Gate

I cringe as soon as we leave airport security, dreading what's about to happen. But it's too late to warn my kids since they've already started walking to the gate.

Well, my seven-year-old son, Justin, is actually *running*, not walking. That's the problem. He wants to catch up to his sister who unexpectedly stops to adjust her backpack—

Whack!

Justin slams right into Emily, full force.

"Ow! Watch where you're going." Emily lets go of the luggage handle and waggles her arms frantically to regain balance.

"Well, you didn't have to stop!" he shouts and waits until she turns away before sticking out his tongue.

By this time, I've caught up with them, and Emily is dragging her feet like she's exhausted from finishing a race. "Mommy, I'm tired. Where's our gate?"

"At the far end of the airport."

Lucky us, one of the last gates.

"No way! All the way at the end?" Justin scowls at me like it's my fault. "That's too far."

"This place is humongous." Emily sits on her luggage and dramatically sighs. "I've already walked a lot. And my backpack is getting heavy."

Enough!

We just dealt with TSA chaos, and now I'm stuck listening to complaining kids.

"Why can't we go on those people moving thingies or whatever you call it?" Justin asks.

Now that's clever thinking. Unfortunately, I only see an empty moving walkway with an "out of order" sign draped across its entrance.

"Good idea, but it's not working. We have to walk. Come on, kids, let's make the best of this situation."

Suddenly, my competitive son has a spark of energy. "I know! Let's race to that pole over there. Ready, go!" Without waiting, he sprints ahead, his backpack bouncing as he darts through groups of people standing everywhere.

Emily follows, yelling from behind. "Hey, I wasn't ready!"

Uh-oh. Racing in a packed airport? Not the best plan.

Dreading someone might get hurt, I hurry after them, flinching as they plow into waiting passengers blocking the aisle. "So sorry," I say to the innocent bystanders, and "watch it!" to my kids, but Emily and Justin are oblivious to the disruption they're causing.

"I win! I win!" Justin cheers, skipping around the pole and pumping his fists in the air.

"You cheated." This time Emily is the one sticking out her tongue, but in front of his gloating face.

Once I catch up, I nudge them away from travelers waiting to board. "You shouldn't race when it's crowded. And we need to stay out of the way. These people are about to get on their plane."

"Mo-mmmyyyy, why can't this be our gate?" Emily asks in a high-pitched voice that makes my insides shiver. "Not fair. I wish this plane was going to New Jersey instead of this place." Staring blankly at the gate sign, she pauses and tries to read the city's complicated name. "Al-bu... Al-bu..."

"It's tricky. Albuquerque."

"Whatever," she says with an exaggerated eye roll. "I just don't want to keep walking."

Complain, complain. This is not fun. I've got to turn this around.

Flipping my head from side to side, I look for inspiration. But in every direction I only see countless people traveling to various destinations.

That's it.

"Hey, let's play a traveling game on the way to our gate."

"Cool," my game-loving son says.

"A what?" Emily asks, raising her eyebrows.

Ignoring her skepticism, I continue with my impromptu plan. "It's called Ooh, Where Do You Want to Go? Here's how we play." I pause to build anticipation, but more importantly to give myself time to figure out what the heck we're going to do.

"See how everyone is traveling to different places? Let's have fun and decide where we want to visit. Our flight doesn't leave for a while, so there's plenty of time. We'll stop at each gate, read where the plane's heading, and then decide if we want to go there."

Emily shoots her hand in the air. "I have an idea! When we reach our gate, let's count to three and share our favorite place."

Laughing, she points to the Albuquerque sign. "This one's easy. Don't want to go there. I can't even pronounce it."

Justin thrusts out both hands and flips his thumbs down. "Nope. Never heard of it."

Two pairs of eyes stare at me, awaiting my response.

"Well, Albuquerque is in New Mexico near Santa Fe. And I've always wanted to visit. So, I give it two thumbs up."

"Guess you'll have to go alone," Emily says, chuckling. "Onward to the next gate!"

"I'll get there first! I'm as fast as a jet." Justin propels forward with one arm clutching his suitcase handle, and the other stretched out like a wing.

"Please, don't bump into anyone," I plead as my kids morph into planes that carefully weave in and out of the crowd.

Suddenly, Justin stops, but this time they're paying attention and avoid another sibling collision. "Wait, what about those gates on the other side?"

Before I can reply, Emily takes over explaining additional rules. "We'll read from over here. Otherwise, we'll go back and forth a zillion times. That one's Los Angeles. Yes, yes, yes! I *love* that place!"

"Disneyland!" Justin squeals. Instantly, he lifts his knees high and marches in a circle, singing the "Mickey Mouse March" song.

"Who's the leader of the club
That's made for you and me?
M-I-C-K-E-Y
M-O-U-S-E."

"Hmm, Los Angeles?" I say. "Do I want to see Mickey Mouse again?" After puzzling looks from my Disney-loving kids, I joyfully respond with a new verse to the song.

"Y-E-S for

M-I-C-K-E-Y

M-O-U-S-E."

Justin zooms ahead, shouting over his shoulder, "My turn to read the next one." In a few yards, he stops and gazes at the sign. Gently, I hold back Emily and press my lips together. Fortunately, she follows my cue and is quiet while her brother tries to pronounce the next place.

"B-o-st-on. Bos-ton. Oh, Boston! Like the Boston Red Sox. Yeah, I like this team. I'll go there."

Emily and I giggle, nodding in agreement.

Justin clutches his sister's hand. "Come on! Let's visit the next place."

"Wait a second," I say. "Don't forget the gate on the other side. How about Chicago—"

"NO!" Justin is so loud that several people turn around and stare.

"Huh? What's wrong with Chicago?" Emily asks.

"That's where the Chicago Blackhawks play. No way! San Jose Sharks fans do not like the Blackhawks. I am *not* going to Chicago."

Emily and I burst into laughter, and I hug my die-hard hockey fan. "Okay, I won't take you to Chicago, but I'll go. That's one of my favorite cities."

Not having any strong feelings about Chicago, Emily looks at us before choosing sides. "Sorry, Justin, I'll go too." Then she takes his hand, and they skip to the next gate.

Eventually, after we virtually visit many cities throughout the United States, we reach the end of the terminal. Justin darts ahead because it's his turn to read. When we join him, he's already adamantly shaking his head. "New Ark. Nah, that sounds silly. I'll skip it."

"You're so funny." Emily says. "First of all, it's called Newark, not New Ark. And second of all, we *are* going there. That's Grandma's airport, and this is our gate."

"Oops, just kidding. I *do* want to go there."

"Me too." I ruffle his hair and give another big hug. "And I'll even go to a place called New Ark."

"Me three!" Emily joins our embrace and then quickly pulls away. "Don't forget the second part of the game. My part! On three, shout your favorite place to visit. Ready? One, two, three!"

"Newark!" Justin and I cheer at the same time. We've been counting down the days until our family reunion, and hooray, it's finally here.

A second later, Emily chuckles. "My favorite place is New Ark."

7

WHEN YOU WISH UPON A STAR

Assigning Chores with an Odd-Even Reward System

Any minute now, one of my kids will ask my least favorite question. Who will say it today? Justin, my seven-year-old son or—

"When's dinner?"

And there we have it. This evening's inquirer is Emily, who is now standing next to me in our kitchen, tapping my arm.

Yup, preparing dinner is one more thing on my never-ending to-do list. It's hard enough squeezing in time, but it's especially challenging as a single mom where there isn't another adult to help.

"Well..." I scratch my head and peer at my daughter. "The cook just called and can't come, so—"

"Mommy, stop joking." Emily cuts me off with a sharp look.

"You're right. It's just little ol' me. Hold on while I grab my chef hat."

"Come on. I'm really hungry. How much longer?" She shifts to her other leg and finally blinks.

"Let's see ... working alone with everything I need to do ... at least an hour—"

"An HOUR!" Justin looks up from his homework and slams his fist on the table. "I'm starving."

No kidding. I wish someone could help. Like the two people glaring at me.

Not sure how to respond, I walk to the sink and wash my hands to start making dinner. As I glance at my tense reflection in the window, I exhale deeply to release some frustration, and I'm bombarded with thoughts.

Why can't they help? I know they're busy. But I'm busy too.

The cool water pours over my fingers and invigorates my confidence.

They should help. And will! Yeah, starting today. But I need a system.

While I dry my hands, I briskly turn around and look at my kids who are still frowning. "How about I make it less than an hour?"

"Now we're talking," Emily says with delight.

"Want us to time you, so you'll move faster?" Justin asks, glancing at the clock and grabbing a pencil.

Emily's eyes sparkle. "Let's eat out!"

Apparently today is not the day for successful telepathic communication with my kids.

Trying to keep a calm demeanor, I merely shrug and shake my head. "No, I'd rather eat at home and save money."

The room is quiet as they wait for my next move, glancing nervously at each other and then looking at me.

"You both are big, right?"

Justin's face lights up. "Yup, I'm seven."

"Hel-lo, I'm nine. Um, where is this going?" asks my older and more skeptical child.

I motion for Emily to join me at the kitchen table with Justin. If nothing else, this gives me more time to think of a plan. "You're learning lots at school. But what do I teach you as your Mommy-teacher?"

"Real. World. Living." Emily's statement comes out in a robotic voice as if she pushed a preprogrammed button.

"Yes, skills you'll use in college and later in life. And now you're old enough to help get dinner ready."

Justin drops his pencil. "WHAT?"

"Humph. I knew something was going on," Emily mutters.

"We're a family, so everyone needs to help." Even though my voice sounds shaky, I refuse to accept defeat. To keep calm, I breathe in and out deeply while my eyes gaze ahead at the calendar hanging on the fridge.

Inhale, exhale, inhale, exhale. Odd date, even date, odd date, even date.

"Hel-lo, Earth to Mommy." Emily's waving arms momentarily shift my gaze.

Odd, even, odd, even. Emily, Justin, Emily, Justin. Yes, that's my system!

On the next exhalation, I jolt up and get the calendar, ignoring their piercing, silent stares. "Have you ever played the Odd-Even game?"

Justin shakes his head.

"Of course not, I just made it up. Look at the month. See, all these dates are either odd or even numbers. What is today's date?"

"The first," Justin announces as if he'll earn extra points for his answer.

"What kind of number is it?"

"Odd," Emily says.

"Yes, today is the first, an odd number. Tomorrow is the second, even. We have two kinds of numbers like we have two kids. So, one of you will be odd—"

"Me! I'm odd," my seven-year-old son squeals, loving anything associated with his age.

I snatch my laptop from the nearby counter to create a chart. After opening a new document, I insert a table with three columns and type their names. "What do we eat before the main meal? This will be the first chore."

"Chores? Ugh." Emily groans.

"Salad. We eat salad," Justin says.

"Yes, and this chore is super cool because you'll use a dinner knife to cut veggies." I type "Make salad" and hope my comment provokes excitement.

Hah, like that will happen!

"Guess another chore." To provide a hint, I jump up and grab a fork, spoon, and knife. "Set the —"

"Table. At least this chore is much better," Emily grumbles as I add it to our chart.

"Wait a second. How is this fun?" Justin asks, squirming in his chair.

"It's an Odd-Even game to figure out your chore. And, we'll also play our favorite music, so we can dance while we work."

Unfortunately, this prompts little reaction. *I better up the ante.*

"And each chore earns a star—"

"Now we're talking." Emily hoists up taller in her seat. "What's a star worth? A quarter? Ooh, a dollar!"

Really? That's some major inflation!

"Every ten stars equals a reward." Immediately, I start thinking of enticing items while I open a new document to type a list. "You can choose a restaurant when we eat out. Decide which movie we'll see. Bake cookies or another treat. Or go out for ice cream. These are a few ideas, and we can add to it."

"Oh, that sounds good!" Justin exclaims.

"I guess," Emily says, unable to hide her smile.

"Now let's create an Odd-Even Days Chores chart. For each task, you'll be either odd or even. When it's time to prepare dinner, you'll check the calendar to see if it's an odd or even day. Then you'll look at the chart to see which chore you're doing."

"Today is the first, an odd day," Emily mumbles under her breath. With deep concentration, she studies the calendar and mischievously grins. "Justin should make the salads when it's an odd day because he loves odd numbers *and* he loves eating salad."

Justin beams as if he received the MVP trophy, and her smirk widens.

I continue explaining. "You'll go back and forth between making the salad and setting the table, depending upon your odd or even task. But sometimes you'll have to do the same chore two days in a row. Know why?"

This is more of a rhetorical question, so I wasn't expecting a response, but Emily is quick to answer. "Yeah, when a month has thirty-one days, like this month, we go from October thirty-*first* to November *first*."

"Correct. When this happens, you'll repeat the odd day chore. Justin will make the salad and Emily will set the table."

Aha, that's her plan!

Justin jumps around cheering about the possibility of doing his preferred task for two consecutive days.

Meanwhile, I whisper in Emily's ear. "Clever thinking assigning odd to the chore you don't like."

She bites her lip and blushes a soft shade of red.

Keeping us focused, I turn my laptop so they can see the Odd-Even Days Chores chart. "So, what will you do when I say it's time to help with dinner?"

"Run in the other direction." Justin giggles.

"Then I'll have to chase you," I say, laughing and tickling him.

Ignoring her brother, Emily says matter-of-factly, "First, look at the calendar to see if it's an odd or even day. Then look at the chart for the chore. Today is odd."

"Oh yeah, salad!" Justin slides off his chair and high fives us on the way to the fridge.

Emily rubs her fingers together and clears her throat. "Ahem, what about the star-earning part?"

I insert another table, type their names at the top, and show Emily the screen. "Here's your star chart."

"Hey, Justin, you should come here and listen to Mommy. This is the best part. Stars!"

So much for two kids wanting to eat right away.

"Right now, the chart is empty, but as I was saying, you'll earn a star for each chore. And this will soon get filled with many stars. I'll draw ten stars per line, so you can easily see when you've earned enough for a reward. When you trade them in, I'll write the reward on that row of stars."

"What are we waiting for? Let's come up with more chores," Emily exclaims, all bubbly.

Star Chart

Emily	Justin
☆ Bake cookies ☆ movie ☆ ☆ ☆ ☆ ☆ ☆ ☆ ☆ ☆	☆ Indian restaurant ☆ ice cream ☆ ☆ ☆ ☆ ☆ ☆

"Huh?" Justin looks at his sister like she's speaking some foreign language.

"Trust me, this is good." She leans over and taps the laptop.

Wow, I wasn't expecting this reaction. Since I'm caught off guard, I try to spontaneously think of additional tasks while adding several more rows. "How about help clean up after dinner? One person clears and wipes the table. The other puts dishes in the dishwasher."

"Nice. What else?" Emily asks. "I want to earn lots of stars for baking and going to the movies."

"Yeah, and I want to use them for eating out. Indian food!" Justin looks around the kitchen for more tasks. "How about taking out the garbage?"

"Don't forget recycling," Emily adds.

Why didn't I think of a reward system earlier?

"Ooh, I have another one! We can help you make dinner," she exclaims.

Wow, my girl who hates cooking is suddenly eager for me to start a culinary school.

Odd-Even Days Chores		
Chore	Emily	Justin
Make salad	Even	Odd
Set the table	Odd	Even
Clear and wipe table	Even	Odd
Put dishes in dishwasher	Odd	Even
Take out garbage	Even	Odd
Take out recycling	Odd	Even
Help make dinner	Any day	Any day

"Fabulous idea. That reminds me of something. Before you go to college, I want you to know at least ten recipes. But I'll explain that when you're in high sch—"

"That's enough chores!" Emily snaps, and she closes my laptop.

"Let's start dinner. Any suggestions?"

"Oh, yeah" Justin leaps off his chair and prances around the table. "Pisghetti, spaghetti! Pisghetti, spaghetti!"

While I grab three aprons, Emily skips to get our favorite Disney music, and Justin runs to the cabinet to take out the pasta.

Part II

Oh No, My Child is Distressed

8

PLEASE, JUST ONE NIGHT OF SLEEP

Making a Child Feel Secure at Night

I jolt out of bed from a deep sleep, hearing my two-year-old daughter's familiar scream. "M-m-mommy! B-b-binky!"

Not again. Please, just one night of sleep.

Uh-oh, I don't want Emily also waking up Justin, my newborn son. Without waiting another moment, I sprint down the hall to find her missing pacifier. Thankfully, she reduces her cry to a low groan as I fly through her doorway.

"M-m-more b-b-binky," Emily sobs, reaching over her crib toward her binky savior—me.

So here I am, once again, standing in her room half asleep. I take a deep breath and speak slowly to control my frustration. "Emily, nighttime is sleep time. It's time to sleep."

As if on autopilot from this recurring routine, I pat her mattress in the dark and place the lost pacifier in her mouth. "Night, night. Go to sleep. I'll see you in the morning." Before leaving, I listen to the peaceful sucking sounds as she settles down.

On the way back to my bed, I tiptoe past Justin's room, who fortunately slept through the missing binky drama.

Then the realization hits.

Yeeks!

If Emily has four screaming episodes per night, that's around fifteen hundred binky runs a year. And with two kids, it could be twice this number.

That's nearly three thousand times per year!

I shudder.

Despite another sleep-deprived night, the next morning I bounce out of bed with an idea: multiple pacifiers. During Justin's early morning feeding, I'm excited to share my plan.

"Ooh, tonight your big sister will go to sleep with lots of binkies. All over her crib. When she loses one, no big deal. She'll reach over and plop another in her mouth. Justin, isn't that a great idea?"

He grins and coos.

"Yes, it should be a *big* success." I wiggle his chubby legs and gurgle on his tummy, which makes him giggle. With Justin cradled in my arms, I stride into Emily's room and flip on the light. "Good morning, sunshine!"

Emily rubs her eyes, a pacifier dangling from her mouth. When she sees us standing over her crib, she yanks out her binky and squeals, "Mommy! Baby Justin!"

"Ready to play with your friends at preschool?"

"Yay!"

I put Justin down to lift my independent girl out of her crib. She squirms and runs to the dresser to choose an outfit. We dart around the house getting ready, and two hours later I manage to get the three of us into the car.

The rest of the morning flies by, taking care of Justin and squeezing in a few household chores during his nap. Before too long, it's time to pick up Emily and juggle the afternoon and evening rituals with two kids.

By Emily's bedtime, I'm eager about implementing my sure-to-succeed multiple pacifier plan. Going from room to room, I go on a binky hunt, gathering as many pacifiers as I can find. Enough for an entire daycare center! Pacifiers with Minnie Mouse, Mickey Mouse, Donald Duck, Winnie the Pooh, Tigger, and a butterfly, as well as pink, blue, red, turquoise, yellow, green, and purple ones. A whole conglomeration. A bundle of binkies!

With pacifiers bulging out of my pockets, I carry Emily to her room and read a story. Tonight, after I lower her into the crib, *I'm the one squealing.* "Look what I have!" Promptly, I pull out a fistful of pacifiers, strategically positioning them around my mesmerized little girl.

"Yay, binky, binky!" Emily cheers and plops Minnie Mouse in her mouth.

"Lots and lots of binkies," I say, waving my hands as more magically appear and fill her crib. What could be better!

Putting my plan into action, I take her hand, and we feel around for pacifiers. "Big girls get their binkies. And Emily is a big girl."

She removes her pacifier and exclaims, "Big girl!"

"Yes. Remember, big girl Emily can get her binky. No more crying for Mommy. See you in the morning." I blow a kiss, wait for her to blow it back, turn off the light, and close her door. With a smug look, I tiptoe down the hall past Justin's room.

Hooray, a night of sleep!

Or so I think.

In the middle of the night, I wake up startled, like someone splashed cold water on my face.

"W-a-a-a-a-a-ah!"

Not again.

Before the second wave of screams, I sprint to her room, hoping to avoid a crying domino effect with both kids.

"Emily," I say with as much empathy as I can summon.

"M-m-mommy! B-b-binky!"

Breathing deeply, I try to keep my cool. "Emily is a big girl. And big girls find their binkies." Yawning, I take her hand, and we feel for pacifiers. "Here, and here, and here. Lots!"

Emily snatches the closest one. Then with rapid sucking sounds she lies down while I tiptoe out of her room, grumbling under my breath.

And that was just the prelude.

Tonight, Emily screeches five times. *Five!* She even wakes up Justin, so I'm juggling two sobbing kids during the wee hours.

There goes my sure-to-succeed multiple pacifier plan.

This morning, I feel especially ragged and barely make it through the day. But I'm determined to come up with a new strategy. One that works! Right now, though, I have no idea what to do.

Later in the evening, after reading Emily a story, I lower her into the crib. Desperately, I look at Raggedy Ann, Brown Bear, and the other stuffed animals who protectively encircle my daughter. By Emily's head, and nearly as big as her, is Mama Doll, with friendly eyes and an endearing smile.

Of course.

Beaming, I swoop up the binkies and place them between Mama Doll's legs. "Mama Doll is Mommy's helper. She keeps your binkies safe."

Emily happily nods.

"When you wake up, you'll go to Mama Doll for a binky. She has lots for Emily."

Leaning closer, I cross my fingers tightly behind my back. "If you wake up, who has your binkies?"

Emily twists her body and stretches her hand to Mama Doll.

So far so good, but I need a better test.

Without any warning, I pry the pink butterfly from Emily's mouth and hide it behind my back. Then I tighten my crossed fingers and wait.

Emily stares at me and then Mama Doll. Slowly, she grins and reaches over, taking a binky from Mama Doll's lap. Right away, she plops Donald Duck in her mouth.

"Hooray for big girl Emily!"

Still smiling, she pats Mama Doll's leg.

"Mommy loves Emily *and* Mama Doll." I purse my lips, grab a kiss, and throw one to Emily who catches it and blows it back. Then she points to Mama Doll. Yes, Mama Doll also needs a goodnight kiss, so I toss another one. Emily pivots her bubbly cheeks and watches the kiss land on her friend.

"Night night, my big girl and Mama Doll." I tiptoe past Justin's room and collapse on my bed where I dream of Mama Doll and dancing binkies.

And sleep soundly all night long.

9

LET'S FLY THE PLANE!

Gaining Control to Tackle a Fear

"M-m-mommy," my five-year-old daughter cries, sinking deeper into the plane's aisle seat. While we wait for the other passengers to board, her chest quivers with each shallow breath.

Poor kid. Just watching her makes me anxious. "Here, Emily, hold my hand." She grabs my fingers and squeezes so tightly that our knuckles turn white.

Oh my, can she grip any harder?

I try to wiggle my fingers free but eventually give up.

Meanwhile, my three-year-old son peers out the plane's window. As if under a hypnotic trance, Justin watches the luggage load onto the conveyor belt until the last suitcase disappears. "Yippee! I love flying."

Probably not the best thing to announce when his sister is freaking out.

Sure enough, she frowns, leans forward, and glares at him. "Err, I hate flying."

"Emily, guess what? I have a surprise to go with your air sickness pill." Thankfully, she releases her hand from mine.

Phew, my poor fingers get rescued from her tight squeeze.

Reaching over, I search my backpack and find the items strategically placed at the top. "Here ya go," I exclaim, waving bottled water, Dramamine, and crackers like they're prized trophies before I put them in her hands.

Once Emily swallows her pill and gets settled, I pull out another bag of crackers. Justin's face lights up when they magically appear on his lap, and he immediately shovels the food into his mouth. "Yummy! Goldfish crackers."

So much for his snack lasting the flight.

As part of my pre-flying routine, I peer inside the airplane seat pockets for an essential inspection. Yup, motion sickness bags are there. Just in case.

The flight attendants finish getting everything ready, and before long the plane starts backing up. Right on cue, Emily's face goes pale, and she clutches both armrests.

"Oh no! M-m-mommy."

She's got to chill out! What can I do to help her before the Dramamine kicks in?

While the plane speeds down the runway, Emily's panic accelerates equally as fast. My body tenses, and automatically my right foot presses down like it's reaching for the brake.

Hah, like I can actually drive this plane.

Yes, that's it. We'll pretend to fly the plane to give a sense of control.

With a plan and determination, I wrap my fingers around a fictitious steering wheel. "Hold onto your wheel, Emily."

"Huh?"

"Look, I have a make-believe steering wheel to fly this plane. See?" I rock my pretend wheel side to side to spark her imagination.

Even though she remains slumped, Emily sighs and slowly lifts her arms.

To keep up the distraction, I give the next set of flight instructions. "Hold on tight. You want to keep your wheel steady."

It's not obvious that Emily will follow, but luckily she sits up tall, grasps her imaginary wheel, and nods. "Got it."

By now the plane is going faster and getting ready to lift off. Usually, this part jostles our stomachs and makes us wince. But not today. We have a mission: to fly the plane!

I look at Emily and smile. "Ready, wait for it. Up, up, and—"

"Away!" we cheer. The plane ascends at a higher speed, pushing our bodies against the seat, but it doesn't seem to bother Emily who is too busy flying.

"Now pull the wheel toward you. We need the plane to go higher. Woo-hoo! We're going in the sky."

"Up, up, and away!" Emily exclaims, mimicking my movement and enthusiasm. While the airplane climbs toward the clouds, my copilot and I focus on following the plane's motion with our hands. *Uh-oh.*

Suddenly, the plane sharply slants into a turn, and my stomach does somersaults. Time to put our flying game into full gear before her anxiety returns and she gets a full-blown panic attack.

"Whee! The plane is turning, so let's help it." Forcing a smile, I rotate my wheel, and sure enough, Emily grins and follows my swift motion. When the plane levels off, we turn our steering wheels in one smooth gesture and straighten out.

"Whatcha doin'?" Justin asks after enjoying the thrilling ride.

"Flying the plane, silly," Emily says.

"No, *you're* silly." He scowls and resumes looking outside at the puffy clouds.

At that moment, the plane abruptly hits turbulence and jostles us around.

Justin swings his hands in the air and squeals, "Wheeeeee!"

Emily's face turns white, and she gasps, once again clutching both armrests.

So much for our let's-have-fun-and-take-control-of-the-plane technique.

"M-m-mommy," she whimpers, turning a shade of green.

Yeeks! I need another distraction... and quick.

Oh my, this turbulence is pretty jarring, tossing us from side to side. It's like the plane is dancing.

Of course. Emily loves to dance, so that's what we'll do.

Right away, I snap my fingers and bop my head in sync with the rough ride. Even though my stomach drops with the plane's motion, I don't let it stop me. "Look! The plane is dancing, and I'm dancing with it."

Emily glances up and grimaces.

"Join me! Let's dance with the plane." Swaying from side to side, I hold her nearby hand and wave it to the jerky movement. "Oh yeah, we're dancing with the plane."

Luckily, her passion for dancing outweighs her fear, so she exhales deeply and starts bouncing in her seat.

"Look at us, we're dancing with the plane," I say.

"Oh yeah!" Her legs swing as she wiggles her hips and pumps her arms.

While the plane rocks through turbulence, we dance in our seats. And Justin enjoys his thrilling roller coaster ride without noticing us at all.

As we jiggle around, I wink at Emily. "Remember, nothing lasts forever. Even this plane will get tired of dancing, and then the ride will become smooth again. Meanwhile, let's dance with it and have fun."

"Yeah, the plane will get tired." Emily's smile widens, and she stretches into a big yawn as the motion sickness medicine starts affecting her.

"Seems like you're getting sleepy," I say, stroking her hair. She cuddles up next to me and leans on my shoulder.

"It's hard work flying a plane *and* dancing with it," she says softly, closing her eyes.

Kissing her head, I respond with an inner glow, "Yes, indeed."

10

THE SURPRISE IMPROMPTU DANCE PERFORMANCE

Turning Fear into Fun

"I-I-I'm scared," Emily mumbles, curling up closer to me on our living room couch. Even though I can barely hear my five-year-old daughter, her quivering voice provides enough clues, and I know what she's saying. She's terrified.

And who wouldn't be!

In a few days, Emily and her younger brother, Justin, will perform at their preschool's Peter Pan dance recital. No big deal.

Yeah, right.

There will be over one thousand people in a large, professional theater. I better keep the attendance number to myself since I don't want to encourage an anxiety attack.

Instead, I hug her tightly and calmly ask, "What are you telling yourself? What are you thinking?"

Emily hesitates, squirms, and then responds. "It's scary. There will be tons of parents. And they'll all be staring at *me.*"

"Yes, there will be lots of people. But you know what?" I shift her body so we lock eyes.

"What?"

"You're dancing with *many* kids, so they'll be watching everyone. And parents will probably only be looking at their child, not you. I know you usually like getting attention, but I'm just saying."

"Yeah, I guess," she says, giggling.

"And what's the most important thing?"

Emily shrugs. "I dunno. Not fall?"

"To have fun." As we cuddle, I notice a small shadow inching closer.

"M-m-mommy, I'm scared too," whimpers Justin, my three-year-old son.

"Come here, our crocodile dancer." Lifting him onto the couch, I swoop him into our family hug. "It's okay to be scared. Even famous dancers get nervous." I nod at Emily. "What's the most important thing?"

"To have fun!" she exclaims, dramatically waving her arms toward Justin, which elicits a big grin.

"Hey, that gives me an idea. You can practice having fun and perform for me now, here at home."

"Ooh, let's wear our pretty costumes. Justin, follow me." Emily grabs his hand, and they prance around the living room as she talks breathlessly. "Mommy, clean the kitchen. Or do something. We'll set up chairs in the living room. Our stuffed animals will be the pretend parents."

"Yay, like Piggie!" Justin cheers.

"How exciting! Let me know when you're ready."

While I work in the other room on my laptop, I hear chairs dragging across the floor, items dropping with a thud, and the pitter-patter of dancing feet—

Boom!

Uh-oh. No screams, so that's good. But now it's quiet. A little too quiet.

What the heck is going on? Not waiting any longer, I briskly walk toward the commotion. "How's it going? You okay? What was that noise?"

Emily races around the corner, panting. "We're fine. A chair fell. Don't come here!"

"No, don't!" Justin yells even louder.

"All right, I'll stay away." I shudder, wondering what they're doing. Since I don't want to disturb their creative flow, I continue proofreading a document for work.

It doesn't take much longer for them to shout, "Mommy, we're ready!"

"Here I come! I don't want to miss the beginning of the performance."

Not sure what to expect, I stride to the living room where I see chairs lined up next to the couch. At each seat is a stuffed animal: Piggie, Brown Bear, Amanda Panda, Mama Doll, Popcorn the Dog, Riff Raff Giraffe, and many others, all propped up in anticipation for the grand show.

"Wow! It's a full house," I say and then gasp in mock panic. "Oh no, I don't have a ticket."

Emily emerges from their hiding spot, shaking her head. "Silly Mommy. You don't need one."

"Phew! Where should I sit?"

Justin's hand shoots out. "There!"

"Yay! I'm on the couch next to Amanda Panda."

Before I can sit, Peter Pan music blasts, and our living room is transformed into a performance theater. Emily skips out facing me and the rest of the audience, her face as bright as her sparkly costume. "Justin, come here. You're part of the intro," she yells, and runs back to pull out our effervescent crocodile.

"Welcome, Mommy and stuffed animals!" She drops Justin's hand and tap dances so fast that her feet sound like a drum. He does his best to follow but merely bumps into her and is shoved out of the way.

"Hey! Don't push me," he shouts.

"Well, pay attention. You can't mess up," our dance leader says.

"Mommy said to have FUN." Justin stands on his tippy toes to better glare at his sister.

Emily shakes her head and sighs. "Fine, we'll do this." Instantly, she starts prancing like a pony, something that a three-year-old can easily do. Soon Justin's face shines as he frolics in circles until she motions for him to step aside.

"The first act is me." Emily lifts her knees, swings her arms, and starts tapping her feet. All of a sudden, she stomps the ground and collapses on the floor, crying. "Oh no! That's not right. I already made a mistake."

"It's okay, sweetie. Just do your best and enjoy dancing." For encouragement, I lift Amanda Panda, and we waltz around the room before returning to our seats.

Emily wipes her eyes and jumps up, her feet tapping wildly.

"Hooray!" I reach over and make Amanda Panda applaud with me.

"The second act is tumbling," Emily says, catching her breath. "Here's Mr. Crocodile."

From the corner of the living room, Justin marches in with his head held high. He places one hand on his hip and the other around Emily's waist.

"He's gonna do what I'm doing. I mean what I *tell* him to do." Emily gestures him over and points to the ground. On cue, Justin widens his legs, tucks his head, and tumbles over, promptly pulling himself up with outstretched arms and the biggest grin. Next, she points to the end of the room where he tumbles all the way to where I'm sitting.

I swear, his cheeks must hurt from smiling so much.

"Wow, impressive." While I applaud, he runs to his designated spot as indicated by Emily, who takes center stage.

"This is our last act. It's called 'The Surprise,' and we'll do whatever we want, like skipping and jumping." As she bounces back and forth, her ponytail wildly swings. "I'm gonna tap dance, and he'll do something else. Then we'll both do a special ending."

I don't know which is faster, her frenetic talking or her pattering feet.

Not waiting for direction from his dancing sister, Justin jumps up and down. "And this! Mommy, Emily, watch what I'm gonna do!"

Justin runs to the corner and thrusts out his arms. He plunges into several semi-cartwheels and then hoists up his elastic waistband, which has slipped down from all the activity. After he finishes, Emily extends her hand to him and starts skipping toward me. But she's going too fast and he can't keep up, so he shuffles a few steps behind.

When Justin joins her at the front of the living room, they each take a deep bow. "Ta-da, me! Ta-da, Justin!"

As my Peter Pan performers take a final bow, I leap off the couch. "Bravo! That was terrific!"

Beaming, Emily waves at me and the stuffed animals. "See ya at the real performance."

After a round of high fives, I smile and ask, "How do you both feel about the dance recital?"

"I wish we didn't have to wait," Justin says, running into my arms.

"I'm not scared anymore." Giggling, Emily points to our pretend audience. "I changed my mind. Now I want you and *all* the other parents to stare at me and cheer, just like our stuffed animals did."

11

THE SECRET MAGICAL BREATH

Teaching Stress Reduction with Mindful Breathing

Something is wrong.

I sense it the moment I pull into the elementary school's driveway. One look at my kids' sad, subdued faces is all it takes.

During any other typical afternoon pickup, my seven-year-old daughter, Emily, would bounce across the pavement and explode in the car with the latest and greatest second-grade gossip.

Not today.

Now she stands like a statue, staring at the pavement. Even from my driver's seat, I can see her eyelids rapidly blinking to prevent tears from streaming down her face.

While my daughter is withdrawn, Justin is acting out his bad mood. With fiery eyes and clenched fists, he forcefully kicks the air, driving an imaginary soccer ball toward a goal. This is an everyday performance, usually ending in a victory dance.

But this afternoon he's behaving more like a wild animal, baring his teeth and stomping the ground.

Oh my. What's going on?

Inhaling deeply, I push away my work worries to focus on the essential job—being Emily and Justin's mom.

I open my window and wave, not too enthusiastically, just enough so they'll notice me. "Emily and Justin, over here." Immediately, they come to the curb and open the door. Within seconds, their anger and sadness pour into the car, filling it with cascading tears and cries. As they fasten their seatbelts, I turn around to give them my undivided attention.

"You look sad. Who wants to talk first?"

Emily slouches and points to Justin who explodes. "NOT FAIR! We should have won."

"Soccer?" I innocently ask. Watching him pretend to kick a ball into a goal gave that one away.

Justin jerks his head with rage. "Time wasn't up. I SHOT IT IN!"

His high-pitched scream pierces my ears, and instinctively I want to yell back "Stop screeching!" but I don't. *Empathy*, I remind myself.

"Very frustrating, especially since you like to win."

By this point, Emily can't hold back her sadness any longer, and tears gush down her face.

"M-m-mommy, I-I-I w-w-wanted to be her p-p-partner." Between loud, convulsive gasps, she tries to explain what happened while I try my best to understand. "A-A-Alexandra, but she w-w-was with some o-o-other g-g-girl."

More sobs.

"She d-d-doesn't even like her. B-b-but Mrs. J-J-Jones separated us."

Knowing the key players, I decipher her sobbing language as something regarding her best friend, Alexandra, and her teacher, Mrs. Jones.

"That sounds yucky. You and Alexandra do everything together."

This comment ignites another round of bawling from Emily.

Not to be outdone by his sister, Justin shrieks at the top of his lungs, "I HATE SOCCER!"

My body shudders, not only from the loud noise but also because he kicked the seat in front of him, which happens to be right where I'm sitting. It felt like an earthquake tremor. Although he's only five years old, he has one heck of a strong kick.

What a way to start the weekend.

I feel my stress level rise. Obviously, I have to do something because my daughter is hyperventilating and my son is shaking the car.

Thankfully, the school attendant is aware of the commotion and hasn't asked me to drive away. Instead, she gives that sympathetic glance that connotes "I don't envy you." I smile back but really think, *Argh, who wants this.*

Slowly, I take a deep breath and then exhale, like the start of a meditation practice.

Yes, that's what we'll do.

Emily and Justin are too upset to notice me pulling the car into an open parking spot instead of driving away. I turn around in my seat and lean toward them to establish eye contact. "Want to hear a secret?"

Loving a good secret, they look at me with curiosity and nod.

Oh, they have the saddest puppy dog eyes. I want to wave a magic wand and remove all their pain. Except for one small issue. I don't have a magic wand, and it wouldn't help them deal with life's heartaches even if I did.

So I continue with my plan.

"The secret is knowing that life is hard, and sometimes you'll get upset. But you can feel better. Know how?"

Justin glances at Emily, but she merely shrugs, so I keep going. "You need to feel your feelings, which is exactly what you're doing."

Once again their bodies shake as they burst into tears.

Wow, they sure took my advice seriously. Here we go. Round two.

Emily's face collapses into her hands, and she sobs relentlessly. Justin convulses into tears and pounds his seat.

While I encourage my kids, "Good," I actually think, *Not good.*

My heart rate accelerates, but I breathe deeply and try my best to emulate the gentle voice of a guided meditation. "I want you to put your hands on your belly."

Amazingly, and luckily, the calm tone works. Emily places her fingers gently on her stomach, and Justin follows his big sister's lead.

"See your hands go up and down? Wow, it looks like they're on a roller coaster."

Emily giggles and Justin's mouth starts to curve upward into a smile.

"Let's pretend to blow bubbles. Breathe in through your nose and watch your hands on your belly rise. Now blow imaginary bubbles with your mouth, but slowly, so they don't pop, and watch your stomach go down."

If nothing else, this breathing exercise is helping *me* calm down.

"Great job. Keep blowing bubbles and watching your belly."

Justin peers at Emily who is intently blowing bubbles and following her belly's movement. He focuses on his breathing and soon says with surprise, "Mommy, look! My stomach isn't a wild roller coaster anymore."

Thank goodness it's working.

"Wonderful. Now that your breathing is calmer, you can breathe through your nose and watch your hands on your stomach without blowing bubbles." I lean over closer and whisper, "I'll tell you a second secret. Your breath is ma-gi-cal." I let the word "magical" float from my mouth.

"How do you breathe if you're upset? In and out slowly? Or fast?" I begin breathing erratically to provide a hint.

"Fast," Emily says.

"*Super* fast," Justin adds.

"That's right. When you're upset, you breathe super fast. And that makes you feel yucky. Life is hard, but there is a secret to feeling better."

This is a challenging concept, so I make sure they're still with me. Yup, their eyes are locked with mine and hands pressed on their tummies.

"The secret is your breath. It can calm you down. If you're annoyed because of a teacher or angry about a soccer game, put your hands on your belly and pretend to blow bubbles."

Both kids look intensely at their stomach.

"Sharing this secret magical breath is the best gift I can ever give you."

"Huh?" Justin looks up, his face twisted in the most confused expression.

"Yup, better than any game, clothing, or whatever. This magical breath helps you fall asleep. It even helps if you're scared. When do *you* think you can use it?"

"Maybe playing soccer?" Justin asks.

"Absolutely. It makes you feel stronger. And helps you focus when scoring a goal."

"But how can I play soccer if my hands are on my stomach?"

"Great point. You don't actually need to place your hands on your belly. Just blow imaginary bubbles, and feel your stomach rise and fall."

Justin beams as if I handed him the best competitive advantage over his opponents.

"How about during the dance performance?" Emily asks.

"That's a great use. It makes you less scared, so you'll remember the steps and have fun dancing. Now, let's go home and—Oh no! There's a big truck behind our car, trapping us in this spot. I can't believe it. Why did he park here? This is going to take forever, and—"

"Aw, Mommy," Emily says, grinning. "I think you should blow some imaginary bubbles."

12

WINNING THE SPIDER GAME

Tackling Fear Through Desensitization

"One more roller coaster before we go home!" Not waiting for a response, my seven-year-old son, Justin, sprints to their last ride at our local amusement park. Emily runs a few steps behind, trying to keep up with her younger brother.

Then, without warning, he abruptly stops and stands paralyzed, like a freeze-frame in an animated movie.

"Hey, watch out!" Emily shouts, swerving out of the way and barely missing him.

Uh-oh, what's going on?

Despite almost getting hit by his sister, Justin stands frozen, tense and trembling. I rush over and wrap my arms around him. Wow, he looks like he saw a ghost.

"Sweetie, what's the matter? Are you okay?"

With eyes fixed on the ground, Justin sticks out his arm and slowly points upward.

Then I see it.

A huge spider. I mean a *humongous* spider! It's probably six feet wide perched on the Haunted Castle as if ready to leap and attack someone.

Emily looks up, gasps, and grabs my arm until the more practical side of her quickly takes over. She exhales deeply and shakes her head. "Humph. It's only a *fake* spider. Let's go!"

But Justin won't budge.

"C'mon, it's fake. Hurry up. We're running out of time. Mommy's going to make us leave. Just close your eyes, and I'll guide you."

"NO!"

It's pretty obvious that Justin is not walking past this spider.

"Really?" Emily says, this time with an exasperated sigh. "Well then, let's go back to the other roller coaster where it's spider free." Not waiting another moment, Justin darts away with his sister running a few steps behind him.

Later, on the drive home, I can't stop thinking about my son's extreme spider reaction. *Mellow out, Carrie. It's a common fear. But to fake spiders? What happens in middle school? Or high school? Oh no, he'll be teased. Tormented!*

I whack each negative thought like I'm attacking a Whac-A-Mole arcade game. Even though I hate to remind him, I better do something to help him overcome this fear.

"Hey, Justin, why were you afraid of that spider? It wasn't real." I nervously glance in the rearview mirror to see his reaction.

As suspected, his face loses color at the mere mention of the incident.

"Not to freak you out," Emily says, "but it's almost Halloween, and there will be tons of spiders. Sure, fake ones, but they'll be everywhere. And I mean *everywhere* you look."

I'm about to interrupt, but she's talking too fast.

"What are you going to do then? Huh? Hide from Halloween? Disappear the entire month of October?"

Justin cringes.

"Not go trick-or-treating?" Finally she comes up for air, so I jump in and rescue my traumatized son.

"Enough! I think he gets the idea."

But she does have valid points. I must help Justin conquer this fear—at least for *fake* spiders.

When we arrive home, I find and hold up his favorite childhood book, *Miss Spider's Tea Party*. On the cover is a friendly cartoon spider with long eyelashes. "Justin, why doesn't this book scare you?"

"Seriously? You've got to be joking," he says, chuckling all the way to his room.

With Justin out of sight, I turn to Emily and motion her to the computer. "I'm going to show him spider images to make him less scared. We need to find and print one per page. Want to help—"

"Yes!" she exclaims. "Let's use really scary ones."

Hmm, I'm not sure if she's trying to help her brother or not, so I clarify. "Wait, we only want cartoon-looking spiders or this will backfire. Yikes, if we use terrifying images, we'll be doing spider patrol when he's in college."

Emily giggles and grips the mouse, eagerly awaiting my instructions.

"First, search for friendly-looking spiders. Next, copy and paste them into a Word document, one per page, and then print. Here, let's do one together, and then you can take over."

Once Emily is immersed in her spider hunt, I walk to Justin's room and put my arm around him. "Being scared stinks."

He pouts and nods slowly.

"You know, I'm scared of heights. But last summer on vacation in Canada, I managed to walk over a suspension bridge made of rope. Like the terrifying, very high and long ones in the *Indiana Jones* movie."

Justin's eyes widen, and he peers at me. "Blindfolded?"

"I wish. Even though I was terrified, I kept crossing the bridge until I was brave. It wasn't easy and took a while, but I did it, and now high places aren't as scary. How about we play a game to help you get over your fear of spiders?"

"I guess," he mutters, scowling and squirming in my arms.

Wow, he must be petrified. Suggesting a game and no reaction?

"This is what we'll do. You'll stand at the end of the hallway. Then we'll count your steps toward pictures of spiders—"

"HEY! That's NOT a game," he yells and flinches, inspecting my hands.

"Sure it is. It's a bravery game. And the spiders will be fake. We'll start with an easy, friendly image, like *Miss Spider's Tea Party*."

I keep quiet, waiting for him to respond.

"Okay, I guess I can do that."

"Yes, you can. Let's do it now."

Quick, before he changes his mind!

Justin slides off his bed and saunters to the bathroom. He turns around and opens his mouth to say something, like he's about to change his mind. I dart past him and stride down the hall, talking loudly to muffle out anything he might say.

"Emily, here I come. How's it going? You almost done? I'll be there in a few seconds."

With a big smile, Emily runs over and displays her images one at a time. "Look what I did!"

"Great job finding spiders. I really like the top hat on this one. These are all great—Yeeks! There's a picture of a large hairy tarantula. It's terrifying!"

How did this one sneak in?

She peers behind the paper with a big grin. "That's when he gets really brave."

"Forget about spider patrol in college because this picture will scare him to death now." I crumple up the sheet and throw it away. After that horrifying image, I decide to keep her under closer spider supervision.

"We'll start with *Miss Spider's Tea Party*. Please prop up the book by the couch."

Emily skips over and sets up Justin's favorite childhood book while he waits at the other end of the hall, fidgeting.

"Go, Justin, go," I exclaim, clapping my hands. "This one is super easy because it's only *Miss Spider's Tea Party*."

He starts walking. Well, more like strolling, but once he realizes it's safe, he makes it to the couch in fifteen steps.

"Woo-hoo!" Emily and I cheer. Justin beams.

"Excellent. Now the next one," I say, giving Emily another spider image. Justin's smile quickly fades to a scowl, and he drags his feet to the starting point.

"You can do it," Emily says. "This cartoon spider looks so cute with its hat."

After hesitating, Justin starts walking while we count his steps. "One, two, three, four, five, six, seven—"

Then he stops.

To measure his fright, I ask, "How scared are you from one to ten? Ten is the worst."

"A TEN!"

Emily leans over and whispers, "Mommy, a ten? What will he say with the less cute spiders?"

Ignoring her remark, I continue with my spider project. "Justin, what are you telling yourself that makes this the scariest level?"

"It will jump off the paper. Attack! And bite me!"

"Do you *really* believe that? It's fake and on a piece of paper, like the one in *Miss Spider's Tea Party* book."

He's silent and then mutters, "I guess not."

"That's right. It's only a picture, so it can't jump off the page, attack, or bite you. It may look a little blurry from over there, but I promise, this is another friendly, fake, cartoon-looking spider. Now, how scared are you?"

Justin shifts from one leg to the next. "Um, a six."

"Good, you're getting less scared."

"You're about halfway," Emily cheers. "You can do it!"

After another deep breath and fidgeting several times, Justin squints before moving. "Okay, it does look cute like *Miss Spider's Tea Party*. I'll now give it a three on the scary scale," and he walks the remaining distance to the picture.

"Yay! You're winning the spider game," Emily says, throwing her arms around him.

I join their embrace and add, "You're very brave. Congratulations, two points so far."

After motioning for Emily to lead him to the starting point, I flip through the images and place the least scary one on the ground. "Here's the next one."

Justin covers his eyes and takes a step while peering through his fingers.

"Um, Mommy, is that allowed? Can he do that?" Emily asks, running back to the couch.

"Sure, as long as he spreads his fingers and can see the image."

We continue the spider game, counting and cheering as Justin creeps along the hallway toward various spider images. Each time he stops, he assigns a fear number, and we discuss the rationale behind his anxiety until the intensity decreases.

"Last one." I prop up the sixth image.

Hmm, this spider is scarier looking. I better up the ante.

"You walk to this one, and we'll celebrate your bravery by eating out. And you get to choose the restaurant—"

"Yay, Indian food!" Justin races to the start, but it takes a while for him to inch forward, even with his fingers pressed against his eyes. Luckily, we aren't starving because it takes ten minutes to walk to this final image, rating and reasoning through his fear level. Ten minutes!

But he does it.

"You're our brave soldier," I say, ruffling his hair.

"Our brave *spider* soldier," Emily adds, giggling.

Justin's body relaxes in my arms. "Oh yeah, Indian food for the brave spider soldier. Me!"

"You betcha," I say. "Then tomorrow we'll get Halloween costumes."

And do exposure in the store with more fake spiders!

During the week, we visit stores decorated for Halloween. Emily sets up pathways, and Justin walks to plastic spiders, napkins with spider designs, stuffed spider animals, and whatever else we can find. He becomes so brave that he even touches the spiders on these items.

Two weeks after our spider training began, I bring out a surprise. "Look what I have for you. Treats!"

"What is it?" Justin stares at a plate of Oreo cookies that have two M&M's for eyes and eight licorice legs protruding from its cream.

"Spider cookies," I joyfully announce and wait for his reaction.

Emily grins. "Aw, so cute. But they're *spider* cookies, so I guess I get *all* of them."

Justin glances at his sister and the cookies. Then he chuckles, snatches the plate, and shouts with Emily chasing after him, "Nope. This brave spider soldier doesn't think so. They're *all* mine!"

13

WHY-I-LOVE-INDIAN-FOOD-SO-MUCH-THAT-IT'S-THE-ONLY-THING-I-WANT-TO-EAT

Teaching Writing Skills

Thud, thud, thud.

What's that noise? It's an unusual, methodical sound coming from where my kids are doing their homework.

"Stop it, Justin!" Emily yells.

Uh-oh, what's going on?

I swivel around to see my daughter glowering at her eight-year-old brother who is kicking the kitchen table. My initial reaction is to holler, but I notice his stern expression, scowling at a blank piece of paper. Instead, I go over and place my arm around his drooping shoulders.

"What's wrong, sweetie?"

Before he has the chance to respond, Emily clears her throat and answers in her fifth grade know-it-all voice. "He didn't do a good job on his paper, so now he has to write another one. But the only thing he's doing is kicking this table. And it's *really* annoying."

Justin looks up, baring his teeth and shaking his fist. "Not fair! I spent a long time on that stupid thing."

Thud. He kicks the table again, causing everything on it to rattle like an earthquake struck.

Ignoring this small tremor, I slide over a chair and sit next to him. "That must be disappointing. Can I see it?"

After a big sigh, an exaggerated eye roll, and a loud "Humph," Justin searches inside his backpack and pulls out a crumpled paper.

"What did your teacher say?" I do my best to flatten the pages and read aloud Miss Perry's comments. "'Justin, it seems like you had fun on your vacation, but your paper is difficult to follow. You have wonderful ideas, so it's important to organize your thoughts. Please try again, choosing any topic.'"

"I can't write. I'm so dumb."

"That's not true. You are *very* smart and *not* dumb at all." I give him an I-love-you squeeze and look into his disheartened eyes. "This is only one paper. One! It doesn't mean you're stupid or can't write. It means you didn't do well on *this* assignment. You can modify your distorted thinking to something more realistic, like 'Gee, I didn't do a good job on *this* paper, but here's a chance to improve my writing.' Does that make sense?"

"I guess," he mumbles. Then there's a moment of silence before he pounds the table and screams, "I HATE WRITING!"

Even though I calmly respond, "Yeah, writing is hard," my insides are in a frenzy. This is an essential skill no matter what you do in life, and hating writing won't help him learn. I need to make this fun. "Hey, let's play a game."

Actually, I have no idea what we're going to do, but I'm sure I'll figure out something in the next few seconds.

Justin smiles. "What kind of game?"

I hesitate before replying. "A writing one."

His spark of hope plummets. "Hey, that's *not* a game."

"He's right. It's not," Emily says in her sassiest of tones.

"Sure it is. We'll play and then eat out. Guess what type of food?"

Instantly, his eyes light up. "Indian?"

"You betcha."

"No, not again!" This time it's Emily who pounds the table.

"Yay, In-di-an food!" Justin springs off the chair and does his I-love-Indian-food dance, triple stepping side to side. "In-di-an food cha-cha-cha. In-di-an food cha-cha-cha."

That's it. I'll use his Indian food obsession to teach him writing.

"Come over here, my dancer. We're going to play a magical writing game. Sometimes it's easier to write when you talk aloud. It also helps to change the location where you're working and go someplace new. Since it's nice out, let's go in the backyard. Emily, grab a pen and put paper in the clipboard. You'll be the reporter and will interview Justin about . . . "

His eyebrows stretch higher, waiting for me to finish.

"About why he loves Indian food!"

Now that catches my foodie son's attention.

"Ooh, I have an idea. Wait a second." Emily dashes out of the room, and in a flash reappears with our sparkly karaoke microphone. "Your reporter is ready!"

"Great, you're official," I exclaim, gently nudging my kids out the back door. "We need a good title. Any ideas?"

Emily giggles. "Why-I-Like-Indian-Food-So-Much-That-It's-The-Only-Thing-I-Want-To-Eat."

"Oh! Oh!" Justin shouts, jumping up and down. "Let's call it Why-I-LOVE-Indian-Food-So-Much-That-It's-The-Only-Thing-I-Want-To-Eat."

"Nice, because you do love it. Here's how we'll play. Emily, you're the reporter who will ask questions and write his responses. Justin, Reporter Emily will interview you, and then we'll magically turn your responses into a story. Ready?"

Both heads eagerly nod, and I'm not sure who's more excited by their roles.

"Ladies and gentlemen, you're in for a treat," I announce to a pretend crowd in our yard. "Get ready to hear Justin's mouthwatering story called," I pause, trying to remember the correct name.

Luckily, Emily is more than happy to help and recites the long title, "Why-I-Love-Indian-Food-So-Much-That-It's-The-Only-Thing-I-Want-To-Eat."

"Hooray! Go ahead, Reporter Emily. Ask me something," Justin says.

She thrusts the microphone in front of his mouth. For a brief moment there's silence, and then in her typical bubbly way, Emily dramatically speaks. "Why oh why, my brother, do you love Indian food?" Afterward, she grabs my arm and whispers, "Mommy, I *really* want to know."

Justin beams like he's about to disclose a secret. "I love Indian food because it's yummy and delicious."

"But *why?*" This time Emily doesn't appear to be acting. Her strong desire to understand is authentic.

Without hesitating he adds, "There are so many flavors and spices."

I raise my hand. "Miss Reporter Emily, may I ask a question?"

Sighing, she slowly hands over the microphone. "I guess."

Before she changes her mind, I ask Justin, "What does it taste like when you eat your favorite Indian dish—"

"Chicken tikka masala!" Emily blurts out. "It's what he always orders."

Justin closes his eyes and inhales deeply like he's actually savoring the meal. "It melts in my mouth. Then bam, I get a rush of flavors exploding. Kaboom!" His eyes pop open, and he licks his lips.

Impressive. We may be unleashing a powerful writer.

"You're making me hungry," I say, motioning for our reporter to write. "Emily, don't worry about spelling things correctly. He'll use a dictionary later. Justin, here's what you said for the intro paragraph."

I have the worst memory. Thank goodness I took notes.

"I love Indian food because it's yummy and delicious." I pause for Emily to catch up. "There are so many flavors and spices."

The pen taps against the clipboard as she quickly writes. Not looking up, she nods for me to keep going. I slowly continue, leaving time for her to transcribe what I'm saying.

"When I eat chicken tikka masala... it melts in my mouth, and then bam... I get a rush of flavors exploding. Kaboom!" When she finishes writing, I ask Justin, "What else can you say about liking Indian food?"

Grinning, he rubs his belly. "It makes my stomach happy."

"Congratulations. You wrote a well-organized, scrumptious introduction," I say, patting him on the back.

"Yeah!" He exclaims, flashing two thumbs up.

"Emily, may I?" I take the clipboard and pen, and point to the first sentence. Both kids step closer. "A paper starts with a topic sentence, the main idea. Your topic sentence is 'I love Indian food because it's yummy and delicious.' Next, you give more details about why this is true. Great job describing the flavors of your favorite dish. Finally, with the concluding sentence, you repeat your point, 'it makes my stomach happy.'"

Shaking her head, Emily looks at her brother. "I still don't get why you love Indian food so much."

"Here's where he develops reasons to support this intro. Let's keep going."

"I have one! Garlic naan is one of the best foods," Justin exclaims.

"So? What's the big deal about this type of bread?" Emily asks.

"Because it's fun to scoop up all the sauce until it's gone." Justin pauses with a smirk. "It's like licking my plate clean without anyone yelling at me. Garlic naan is the best!"

"Oh, now I get it," Emily says, nodding with a smile.

"Aha! That's why you love it so much." I hand her the clipboard and tap the paper for her to continue transcribing Justin's story. "One of my favorite things is the garlic naan... It's fun to scoop up all the sauce until it's gone... It's like licking my plate clean... without anyone yelling at me... Garlic naan is the best!"

By now, Justin is nearly salivating. "Yeah! In-di-an food cha-cha-cha. In-di-an food cha-cha-cha," he chants, prancing around the yard.

"Come here, you two. I love you so much." I embrace my kids, holding on longer than our usual hugs until Justin starts fidgeting. "Remember this useful magical writing trick of talking aloud. Since it's hard to find an interviewer, you can always pretend you're talking to someone on the phone, like one of your grandparents."

"Yeah, I may not be available," Emily says in her grown-up voice.

"That's true. So, you can do this." I wink, hold a make-believe phone, and begin speaking. "'Grandma, let me tell you why I love Indian food.' Then imagine her asking 'why?'"

"That's so funny." Justin giggles.

"Here, take this clipboard and write your story for Miss Perry. You already have your introduction and one great reason. You love Indian food so much, I'm sure you can come up with a few others. Just follow the same process, writing the topic sentence, explaining more details, and then repeating your point."

"And, what's Mommy's trick? What should you do if you're stuck?" Emily asks.

"Hold a make-believe phone and talk to Grandma," Justin exclaims.

"Yup. You both are great listeners. When you're done writing your reasons, add a conclusion which ties the paper together. Like—"

"You love Indian food so much, it's the only restaurant you ever choose," Emily says, and with a smile, rolls her eyes.

"I could eat Indian food for every meal!"

"Those are great concluding sentences. Make sure to use the dictionary and check your spelling."

Justin darts inside while Emily and I enjoy the gorgeous weather for a little longer. When we go in the house, we see him hunched over the paper, clenching his pencil, and mumbling under his breath. "Grandma, Indian samosas are the best. Why? I'll tell you. They are heaven put into a triangle. So many flavors, and I get to put the spicy sauces on them!"

A while later, Justin hands me his paper. "Ta-da! I'm done."

I can't help commenting as I read. "Wow, this is well organized with compelling reasons. You convinced me that Indian food is delicious. My stomach is growling. Let's go eat!"

Later, once we've ordered food at the Indian restaurant, Justin clears his throat to get the waiter's attention. With passion, he performs a soliloquy as if accepting a Best Actor award.

"I love Indian food so much that it's the only thing I want to eat. It's yummy and delicious. Ahhhh, there are so many flavors and spices. The chicken tikka masala melts in my mouth, and then bam, I get a rush of flavors that explode in my mouth. It makes my stomach so happy!"

The waiter's eyes open wider.

Emily pretends to grip something in her fingers. "Yum! It's fun taking the garlic naan and scooping up all the sauce, every last bit. De-li-cious!"

A smile spreads across our speechless server. As he turns to walk away, he mumbles under his breath, "Wow, they *really* love Indian food."

14

THE DAY WE SCREAMED PROFANITIES WHILE DRIVING TO SYNAGOGUE

Tackling Fear by Challenging the Inner Voice

From out of nowhere, I hear a loud piercing sound.

Oh no! It's my twelve-year-old daughter crying. As I sprint down the hall to Emily's room, her sobbing intensifies and my heart beats faster.

"Sweetie," I say, dropping to the floor and embracing her.

"M-m-m-mom. I can't d-d-do this."

"This" is her Bat Mitzvah. The momentous ceremony when a young Jewish adult leads a two-hour service in English and Hebrew, singing intricate melodies and reading Hebrew calligraphy from the Torah, the Old Testament.

No big deal.

Yeah, right. There will only be hundreds of friends, family, and congregation members critically watching her. Frankly, I was shocked the fear hadn't hit her sooner.

Really though, now? A panic attack? The service starts in less than an hour!

Her timing couldn't be worse.

It takes at least twenty minutes to drive there, and we need to get going. Being late is not an option, especially since she's the star.

I take a deep breath and then another to appear calm. "Sweetie, I know this is scary. But you'll do a fantastic job. Let's finish getting ready. We have to leave in five minutes."

"I-I-I-I'm so scared. I-I-I-I don't want to do it. I-I-I-I d-d-don't feel well."

Uh-oh. The clock is ticking, and Emily is in full-blown panic mode.

My jaw clenches tighter, but getting annoyed won't help this situation.

"Um, Mom, is she okay?" With all the commotion, I didn't notice my ten-year-old son standing by the door. Hesitantly, Justin hands his sister a box of tissues.

How sweet. Ordinarily, on any other day, I'd embrace my kids in a tight hug. But punctuality wins over treasuring this moment, so I toss aside empathy and switch to business mode.

"She's scared but will be fine. We're going to be late. Everyone, in the car!"

Emily stares in disbelief while I yank her off the floor and drag her down the hall.

All right, I won't win the Most Empathetic Mom award, but I have no choice. I must gain control. We need to arrive before the service begins... which is soon.

"Let's go!" Whipping around, I grab our items by the door. "Come on. We'll talk during the drive."

Actually, I have no idea how to help her, but I better figure out something... and quickly.

Justin leads his trembling sister to the passenger seat and sits in the back. Tears stream down Emily's cheeks as she gulps for air while my fingers clutch the steering wheel for support.

Lovely, now what should I do? The Bat Mitzvah handbook needs to add tips for dealing with massive freak-outs!

Panic attacks are no fun. I shudder and then grin, recalling how I once coped.

"Hey, kids, remember last year my friend Kate and I hiked along the Hawaiian volcano cliffs? There were drop-offs on both sides and I had to scramble over rocks. I panicked. I mean, I thoroughly freaked out, screaming, clutching the ground, and refusing to move."

"Yup, you hate heights and climbing." Justin chuckles, and even Emily's expression slightly softens.

"Kate's a therapist, so she used her psychology magic. We talked about my fears and then, amazingly, I managed to walk across the ledges without shrieking. Emily, what's scary about your Bat Mitzvah?"

There's silence before she responds in a quivering voice. "I'm scared that I'll forget the Hebrew melodies and prayers. I'll be standing there while everyone stares at me. And they'll think I'm an idiot. Then when everyone's laughing, I'll faint or puke all over the rabbi, cantor, and me."

"Well, the rabbi and cantor will jump out of the way," I tease. *Too soon? Probably.* Emily juts out her chin and glares at me.

"Seriously, sweetie, these are only distorted, exaggerated thoughts. The fancy terms are Catastrophizing or Making a Mountain Out of a Molehill. It's normal, but it doesn't feel great, does it?"

Emily shakes her head.

"When we catastrophize, we see the worst outcomes even though they're unlikely to happen. Do you *really* think you'll forget what you've intensely studied for the past year? And do you *really* think you'll do something dramatic like faint or puke?"

After a few moments, Emily snickers. "Probably not."

"Also, big whoop if you forget something. That's why the cantor stands next to every kid, to chant along when someone needs help."

Emily sighs deeply and looks up.

"Let's replace these bad thoughts with more realistic ones. For instance, you can think, 'I've done a great job preparing and am more than ready. Yes, I will probably make some mistakes, but that's okay and expected. If or when that happens, I'll just keep going.'"

She sighs again, but her face remains ashen.

Yikes, only ten more minutes! Time to crank up my technique.

"We're going to do something, but first you need to sit confidently." To set an example, I elongate my spine like a ballerina. Emily raises her head and lifts herself up, sitting higher on the seat.

"Kate told me a secret when I freaked out at the volcano edges. She said that everyone has an inner negative Voice that comments on your life. This Voice is like a bully who uses mean, critical, or scary thoughts. But guess what? You don't have to listen."

Emily leans closer, listening more intently.

"When this Voice becomes a troublemaker, you need to push back and yell at it. The stronger the fear, the harsher you want to be. So go ahead, tell off your mean, ridiculous Voice."

"Dumb Voice," Emily mumbles quietly.

"Really? No way! You can do better than that. Firmly tell it to stop."

"Stop!" This time Emily is a little louder.

Oh no, this isn't working! She's still upset. Hey, I have an idea. But how sacrilegious of me. Especially since we're driving to a religious event. I probably shouldn't do it. But drastic times call for drastic measures. Carrie, just do it!

Cringing, I shrug and yell, "Fuck off, Voice!"

Once again, Emily's body shakes, but this time from giggling.

"The Voice's critical thoughts are hurting your self-esteem, so you need to be extreme. Go ahead and say it. 'Fuck off, stupid Voice!'"

With a smirk, Emily looks at me and raises her eyebrows. "Fuck off, stupid Voice!"

Shocking? Yeah, but my daughter is regaining control of her negative thoughts and calming down.

From the rearview mirror, I see Justin's jaw drop. "Can I say it too? Can I?"

"Sure, go ahead."

Justin inhales and bellows until his face turns bright red. "Fuuuuuuuuuuuuuuck off, Voice!"

While driving the remaining miles to one of the most sacred Jewish events, our car fills with profanities . . . and laughter.

As we get closer, I flip my head toward Emily and ask, "Feel better?"

She nods with a big grin.

"Remember, we only say 'fuck' in extreme situations, like being terrified right before your Bat Mitzvah. And only when I give you permission. Now, let's roll down our windows to purify this car."

The windows squeak open and close while we slide into the spot reserved for the guest of honor. Emily's friends skip toward the car, waving energetically, and my once-petrified daughter can't get out fast enough to join everyone.

Turning around, I wink at Justin. "Wow, only two more years until *your* Bar Mitzvah."

For a second, his face turns white. Then with a smirk, he leans closer to me. "Fuck off, Voice!" he says in a soft, pious voice because, after all, we're in the synagogue's parking lot.

Part III

Uh-Oh, My Child is Bored

15

ONE, THREE, FIVE, SEVEN, NINE. ODD NUMBERS ARE MIGHTY FINE

Gas Station Guessing Game

It's like any other ordinary drive home from school until Emily, my six-year-old daughter, points to the dashboard. "Mommy, what's that light?"

Uh-oh, not good. Which car warning symbol is it this time?

My eyes glance at the console, and immediately I think the worst. *Engine issues? Brake problems? Bad battery?* Hah, like I know what that weird icon on the dashboard means.

"Where? What light?" Since my four-year-old son never wants to miss anything, Justin tries to peer around the front seat to see the excitement.

This is not how I want to end the day.

Inhaling deeply, I look down and exhale a second later. Phew, false alarm. It's only the low fuel indicator.

"No need to worry. This light is letting me know that we're almost out of gas. The car is saying, 'I am hungry. Time to visit the gas station.'"

"That's so funny. Carol's hungry." Justin giggles.

I wink in the rearview mirror at my child who likes naming our car. "Yup, Carol the Camry wants to eat."

"Hel-lo. *I'm* the one who's hungry. Get gas tomorrow!" Emily demands.

"Nope, we need gas when the light comes on." *Or before,* I remind myself.

"Mo-mmyyyy, why can't you get gas later?" Emily asks with a high-pitched whine.

"We're getting gas now, and lucky for us there's a station across the street."

Thank goodness. It's enough with her whining!

"Humph." Emily slouches deeper in her seat, refusing to give up. "I want to go home."

Justin glares at his sister like she's starving her child. "Did you hear Mommy? Carol needs to eat."

We pull into the gas station, and unfortunately there's a line. I turn around to reassure my daughter. "It shouldn't be long before our turn."

But this doesn't help the situation. Emily locks eyes with mine, scrunches her face, and says, "I am very, *very* hungry."

"Hmm, are you *very* hungry like the caterpillar?" I ask, raising my eyebrows playfully.

"Oh, I *love* that book!" Justin exclaims.

Emily, who also likes *The Very Hungry Caterpillar*, breaks into a slight smile, and her dull eyes begin to sparkle. She rubs her stomach, clears her throat, and dramatically starts reciting the book from memory. "Very, very hungry. So hungry I could eat one apple, two pears, three plums—"

"Four strawberries!" Justin shouts the number for his age and then nods at Emily to continue.

"And five oranges." She waves her hand and five pink nails sparkle in the sunlight.

"Nice job, and hooray, now it's our turn," I say with relief and drive forward to the open pump.

"Ugh, we still have to wait for the stupid gas to finish," Emily groans again. "Did you hear that? My stomach is growling. It's saying 'feed me!'"

No more complaining! She needs a distraction.

"You know what? All those *Very Hungry Caterpillar* numbers give me an idea." I unroll the backseat window, turn off the ignition, and climb out of the car. A second later, my head pokes through their window. "We're going to play a guessing game with numbers."

Justin's face lights up, and he begins chanting. "Num-bers, num-bers, num-bers!"

"Look at the two rows of numbers," I say, pointing to the pump while my kids squirm to see. "The bottom is the gallons of gas that go into the car, and the top is the cost. We won't know Carol's numbers until we're done pumping, so this is a guessing game." I fumble with my credit card and insert it into the pump while pressing the appropriate buttons.

"Um, those are really big numbers. I can't even read them," Justin says with a lot less zeal than his previous energetic chant.

"That's okay. This is an odd-even guessing game. You don't need to read the entire number. Only the last digit. Emily, aren't you learning odd and even numbers at school?"

"Oh yes!" She squeals and bounces in her seat. Good thing she's wearing a seatbelt, or she'd smack her head against the roof of the car.

"My teacher wrote the numbers one to ten on the whiteboard with little lines underneath each number. You know, like one line for one, two lines for two, three lines for three. Then she drew a circle around every two lines, and they were partners. It was so cute. If all lines had a partner, the number was even. But if there was a leftover line, it was an odd number. Those were the lonely numbers. Guess which one's my favorite? Even numbers!"

I start pumping the gas and return to the open car window. "Right, so you and—"

"One, three, five, seven, nine. Odd numbers are mighty fine." Emily sings as fast as the gas meter spins. "Two, four, six, eight. Even numbers we appreciate." By this point, she's nearly hyperventilating. "One, three, five—"

"Em-i-ly, stop!" Justin thrusts out his hand. "Let Mommy finish."

I jump in while I have the chance. "Quick, we have to play before the numbers stop spinning. First, let me explain. All numbers, no matter how small or large, are either odd or even. Want to know a trick?" I keep talking before they have a chance to respond. "You only need to look at the last number, which determines the type. Now, guess if our gas price and the number of gallons will be odd or even. One of you choose odd and the other ev—"

"Even! I'm even," Emily shouts. Then there's a brief moment of silence while she catches her breath, and Justin sits wide-eyed, taking this all in.

"Okay. Justin, you're odd, and don't worry, you'll learn about odd and even numbers later in school."

"Yeah, when you're bigger like me," Emily says.

"Watch the numbers as I feed Carol. When she's full, the numbers will stop spinning."

Justin turns to stare at the pump while Emily leans over to get a better glimpse.

"Odd, odd, odd!" he chants.

"Go even! Go even!" Emily grins at her brother with that I've-got-this look.

For the next few minutes, they cheer nonstop, and the person on the other side of the pump keeps glancing over with a raised eyebrow. Eventually, the numbers stop spinning and the back seat starts squealing.

Luckily, no one is waiting behind us, so I take my time and project my voice like I'm announcing the results of a race. "Here are the final numbers. The cost of gas is twenty-one dollars and sixty-three cents, which ends with a three. Miss Emily, who's learning odd and even numbers in school, what type of number is it?"

"Odd!" Then with less enthusiasm, she says nearly in a whisper, "No fair."

"Oh yeah, mine!" Justin smiles so wide that his teeth show.

"Next, the gallons of gas is fourteen point nine six nine, which ends with a nine. Miss Emily?"

The car is silent except for the faint sound of Emily singing the Odd-Even song. "One, three, five, seven, nine. Odd numbers—Oh, nine!" Her excitement plummets and she scowls. "Hey, no fair. Another odd number."

Justin dances a jig that rocks his car seat from side to side. "Yay, I win again! What's the prize?"

Prize? Nice going, Carrie.

After a brief pause, I confidently respond. "Bragging rights."

He grins, and so does Emily. She may have lost the contest, but at least she's not missing out on a tangible reward.

With the car full of gas, I swing open the door and settle in my seat. "Time to go home because someone else I know is very hungry."

"Let's do it again!" Emily says, forgetting about her growling stomach.

"I promise, in a couple of weeks when the car needs more gas."

Justin chuckles. "You mean, when Carol the Camry is hungry again."

16

THE EYEBROWS-RAISED-HEAD-NODDING SIGNAL

Getting a Server's Attention

"Didn't you hear me?" my seven-year-old daughter asks. "I'm bored. Why can't this place have menus to color? And now I'm thirsty. I need more water."

I cringe as Emily tips her glass upside down, but luckily it's empty, so nothing pours on the restaurant's table.

"Oh yeah? Well, I'm *super* thirsty because we just raced, and I'm the fastest kid in kindergarten. I need to drink lots." To emphasize his point, Justin lifts his glass and guzzles the rest of his water. He wipes the droplets off his mouth and pounds the glass back on the table.

"But I finished my drink before you," Emily says and then glares at me. "Mommy, we really need more water."

"Okay, I'll get the server." I do a little magic and within seconds, the waiter starts walking toward our table.

Justin stares open-mouthed. "Hey, how did you get him to come over without saying anything?"

Emily flips her glass upright and slides it closer to the edge. "How did he know? You didn't raise your hand. We didn't have to wait. You—"

"May I help you?" the waiter asks while Justin gawks, and Emily keeps rambling under her breath.

"More water, please," I say.

The server nods and disappears.

"Really? How did you do that?" Emily hoists herself closer to me like she's about to discover the world's most coveted secret.

Ah yes, beckoning someone to her command is definitely appealing.

A moment later, the server returns with a pitcher, and my kids don't blink as he refills our glasses.

When he leaves, I chuckle and chug some water. "Don't you know? I have magical powers."

"Mommy, you have to tell us," Justin demands, squirming in his seat and scowling at me.

"Fine, I'll share the secret." Pretending we're surrounded by spies, I glance around the room, point to my eyebrows, and whisper, "It's all right here."

"Huh? Your eyes—"

"Shhh! Let her finish." Justin thrusts out his palm to keep his sister quiet.

"Watch closely." I point to my face while raising my eyebrows and lifting my head twice.

"That's it? That's all you do?" Emily shrugs and shifts in her seat.

"Yup. Servers know this secret signal and will come over to find out what you need."

"You mean they learn that in *servers'* school?" By now, Justin is thoroughly dumbfounded.

"Well, sort of. They're taught to watch for the eyebrows-raised-head-nodding signal. See that group of waiters standing in the corner with their backs against the wall, looking at everyone? What do you think they're doing?"

"Waiting for us to signal them?" Justin asks.

Emily bounces in her seat and grips my hand. "Do it, Mommy!"

"Yeah!" Justin's face shines like he's about to watch an impressive magic trick.

Okay, Carrie, nice job setting up this situation.

I look at my eager kids and then at our waiter. Carefully, I raise my eyebrows and nod my head twice. On cue, our server pushes himself off the wall and walks straight toward us.

"He's coming!" Emily says in a loud whisper.

"Wow!" Justin's eyes grow even wider.

"May I help you?" the waiter asks.

At once, Emily inhales sharply, and Justin clasps his mouth with both hands.

Uh-oh. What do we need? Quickly, I glance around our table to find some desired item. "Yes, more napkins, please."

The server nods and leaves while Emily sighs and shudders. "Phew, nice save, Mommy."

"Wow!" Still confused, Justin tries to imitate this signal. He nods at me and then squints, grimaces, blinks, closes his eyes, and wiggles his nose. Everything other than raising his eyebrows.

"Mommy, I think Justin is trying to signal that he wants something from you," Emily says, giggling.

"Yeah, those eyebrows are stubborn and won't go up. Keep practicing. Oh good, here comes our dinner." I push aside items to make room as the waiter delivers moo shu chicken, lemon chicken, broccoli beef, and rice.

"Yummy!" Finally, Justin relaxes his face and focuses on the food.

Yummy indeed. Nothing like a delicious Chinese meal, so I grab the spoons and serve everyone.

Throughout dinner, I notice my son practicing the eyebrows-raised-head-nodding signal. "You want to try it?" I ask.

Right away, he stops chewing. "Really? Can I?"

"Sure, go ahead. Look at our waiter over there. He's the tall one. Lift your head twice and try raising your eyebrows."

After swallowing and sitting up straight, Justin holds himself very still and slowly lifts his head twice. Even though his eyebrows don't quite rise, the server comes over anyway.

"May I help you?" Confused, he looks at Justin, then me, and then Justin again. I guess it's not every day a young child requests his service.

Emily gasps and holds her breath.

"Uh... um... uh..." Justin stutters, his face turning a deeper shade of pink. I'm about to rescue him when he says, "More napkins, please."

He did it!

The server smiles and in a flash returns with a handful of napkins, which he adds to our growing pile, and then briskly walks away.

"Way to go!" Emily squeals and applauds, and I raise my glass to Justin who beams like he won a trophy.

We continue eating and visiting, but our conversation is interrupted when I notice the waiter standing at our table, peering down at us.

"May I help you?" This time our server sighs and shifts his weight to the other leg.

"Um," my guilty son mutters, surveying the table.

Emily coughs, waving her fork back and forth to catch her brother's attention and provide a hint.

"Um, more forks. Please." This time, Justin barely looks up.

"Th-a-nks." I say, turning a simple one-syllable word into three syllables.

When the server leaves, Emily pats Justin on the back.

Oh no, what did I create? An eyebrows-raised-head-nodding maniac!

"Did you signal him again?" I ask, doing my best to stifle a laugh since I don't want to encourage this new habit.

With a big grin, Justin attacks his broccoli beef as more forks materialize on our table.

"Thank you. Thank you very much. We really needed—"

Before I can finish apologizing for Justin's newly acquired addiction, the server darts off.

We continue devouring the food and sharing stories about our day, but soon another shadow appears. This time I hear a foot tapping and then notice the waiter glaring at us.

"What do you want?"

So much for being a mom with two cute kids.

At this point, Justin can't even look at the server.

"More chopsticks, please," Emily says, rescuing her brother.

After mumbling something in Chinese, our waiter reaches in his pocket and plops a handful of chopsticks on the table. He's gone before anyone can utter "thanks."

"Hey, kids, we can't overuse these magical powers. It's not fair to the server or other customers who might need something. Besides, there are only so many things that will fit on our small table."

"But, Mommy," Justin says. "I'm practicing."

By this point, I can't hold back my laughter. "Well then, you did a great job. Look at this big pile of napkins, forks, and chopsticks. I'll give the server a big tip, and I give your eyebrows-raised-head-nodding signaling an A."

Emily balances the last batch of chopsticks on top of the other items and giggles. "An A-*plus!*"

17

HOW LONG BEFORE
OUR TURN?

Making a Game of Waiting in Lines

My eight-year-old daughter pushes open the store's bathroom door, which loudly smacks against the wall. "I've had to go since the food court and pretzel place," Emily says. "I can't wait any longer."

"Wow, that's a long time," I say.

"And so is this line!" Fortunately, Emily abruptly stops before colliding into a group of people waiting, staring at their watches and sighing.

I push us deeper into the small, crowded space, away from the door. We certainly don't want to get hit by someone else storming in with a full bladder.

Justin pokes my side and narrows his eyes. "Err! I'm getting squished. And I don't want to be in here with all these girls. Can I wait outside?"

"No way," I say without hesitating. "Maybe next year when you're seven."

He slumps against the wall and groans. "It's bad enough I'm in the girls' bathroom. Now I'm stuck here even longer."

When I won't budge, Justin's stern expression morphs into a smile, and he switches to his sugary sweet tone. "Please can we go? Pretty pleeeeease?"

He sure looks cute batting his long eyelashes, but I hold my stance. "Nope, we're here, so we'll wait. Besides, it looks like Emily is about to explode, and now I also have to pee."

"Humph," Justin says as he stomps the ground and mutters something under his breath.

"Really, I can hold it 'til we get home," Emily insists. "Come on, let's go." While her words say one thing, her legs squeezing against each other say something else.

So much for having a peeing ally!

Emily jiggles in place, hopping from one foot to the other. "How long before our turn? Why can't bathrooms have signs like Disneyland with the wait time?"

Wait time, yes!

"That gives me an idea. Let's play a guessing game," I exclaim.

The word "game" sparks their attention, but not enough to make Justin stop scowling. "Huh? How is standing in the stupid girls' bathroom a game?"

"Sure it is. Guess how much longer we have to wait—"

"An hour!" he shouts.

Emily's eyes widen. "An hour? This doesn't seem like a good idea."

"I promise it won't take that long."

Yeeks, it better not. In thirty minutes we could be peeing at home.

To distract them and start the game, I delegate tasks. "First, we need some key info in order to guess our wait time. Justin, count the number of stalls. Emily, count the number of people in front of us."

While Emily is eager to push her way through the crowd, my son stares at his sneakers. When he doesn't budge, she reaches out and takes his hand. "Here, come with me," and she leads him up front to do their jobs.

Momentarily, Justin runs back, wiggling two fingers. "Two! Two stalls."

Meanwhile, Emily counts the number of people and announces, "Eight. Wait, two toilets just flushed. Hooray! Now six."

"See, we're already making progress." We do a round of high fives, and then I glance at my watch. "It's two o'clock. We'll guess the wait time from now. Someone needs to remember the time."

Emily motions for Justin to be the timekeeper, and he confirms. "Got it, two o'clock."

I pull my kids into a tight huddle and whisper like a spy sharing a classified mission. "Our goal is to figure out how many minutes until our turn. We'll base it on six people ahead of us. What if there were enough toilets for everyone?"

"The line would go super fast." Justin zooms around our area until I gently pull him back.

"Correct. So, we can determine the wait time by the number of stalls and people."

They nod, and I nudge us forward. "In this bathroom, there are two stalls, so our wait is cut in half. We don't have to wait as long since some will use Stall One and others will use Stall Two." I look at Emily. "This means we can divide the number of people by two. What's six divided by two?"

"Three!" she exclaims and pats Justin's head. "You'll learn division when you're bigger like me."

"Yes, three people for each stall. Now guess the number of minutes someone typically spends."

I'm not a peeing expert, so I actually have no idea.

"Boys are fast. One minute," Justin says.

Emily shakes her head. "No way. Girls take longer. Maybe three minutes."

"Let's use two, which is between your numbers. Some will take longer and others will be quicker, but we're assuming that most women only need two minutes."

"Two minutes to pee or do whatever." Justin giggles.

I waggle my eyebrows, acknowledging his six-year-old humor and then high five my kids again. "Congratulations. We have enough info to figure out the number of minutes until our turn. Three people in each line, needing about two minutes each. That's three times two." I glance at Justin and translate to first-grade math, counting on my fingers. "Three plus three—"

"Six. Easy-peasy," Emily responds.

"Hey, I was gonna say that. Six."

"Yes, we predict a six-minute wait. Guess what? Now there are only two women in front of us. One for each stall. And people have been in there for a while, so it should be less than two minutes until our turn." Sure enough, shortly after I finish talking, both doors swing open.

"Yay, we're next! Mommy, what time is it? Justin, what was the start time?"

"Two o'clock," he says with a salute.

I look at my watch while two pairs of eyes stare at me. "I'll tell you the time when someone comes out. That's when our wait will be over."

Then a toilet flushes and Emily squeals.

"It's now six after two, so that took six minutes. Hey, we were right," I say.

They jump around high fiving each other and cheering, "Our turn! Our turn!"

"Nope, *my* turn," Emily shouts and darts over when one door opens. Before going in, she pokes out her head. "And now it's a zero-minute wait for me."

"Yeah, me too." Justin slides past me, disappearing into the other open stall, and in less than a minute he's done. "Told you. Boys pee fast."

My bladder is about to burst. Thank goodness it's my turn.

On our way out, a woman enters the bathroom with a boy younger than Justin. When he sees the line, he stops and tugs at her sleeve. "Oh no, Mommy, this is gonna take a long time."

Emily looks at the boy, turns around to count the people in line, and pauses a moment. "Don't worry. There are four people in front of you, and there are two stalls. It takes each person about two minutes, so it's only a four-minute wait."

The boy gawks like he's trying to understand a foreign language. I simply shrug and smile while Justin runs out the door. "Race you to the elevator!"

Emily looks at me and chuckles before chasing her brother. "Hey, Mommy, guess how long it will take us?"

18

ARE WE THERE YET?

Keeping Kids Entertained in the Car

Today I wake up expecting my kids to jump on the hotel bed and cheer. "This trip's a blast!" "I'm having the best time!" "Mommy's the greatest!"

Well, maybe they won't give me kudos, but they'll be ecstatically cheerful, euphoric, and downright excited.

Nope.

Instead, nine-year-old Emily and I are standing in a crowded hotel lobby, listening to my son throw a tantrum.

"No more driving! I'm tired of being in the stupid car." Then Justin throws back his head and hollers until his face turns red. "NOOOOOOOO!" Everyone in the lobby turns and stares.

Seriously, can he be any louder?

"Stop it! You're embarrassing me." Emily winces, grabs her luggage, and hurries past us to escape the area. On her way out, she says through clenched teeth, "We. Are. Tired. Of. Driving."

"I don't believe this. We're not even in the car, and you're both already complaining? Let's go!"

While Emily stomps ahead, Justin drags his feet. At this rate, he'll take forever, so I grip his hand, and we forge ahead.

Unfortunately, things don't improve at the car.

When I'm busy loading the trunk, I notice Justin tiptoeing around me. Before I can determine his plan, he sneaks behind Emily and yanks her ponytail.

"Stop!" she screams and lunges to jab him, but he's too quick and darts away. "Mommy, I don't want to be cooped up in the car with my dumb brother."

Thud. I slam the trunk, shake my fist at Justin, and embrace my scowling daughter.

Lovely. Time to try a game I recently read in a magazine.

Before he can provoke any more trouble, I delegate my son a task. "Justin, please get a pen and paper from my bag. We're going to play a game."

"What kind?" he asks, digging in my purse.

"You'll see, and we'll set it up here."

Thank goodness he's calming down, but unfortunately, Emily is still seething.

"HERE? In the hotel parking lot? Oh no!" she yells, glaring at her brother. "People might recognize us. Take off your sweatshirt! Someone may remember you as that screaming kid."

Justin gives me the paper and pen, and slowly removes his sweatshirt. It's barely over his head when Emily tugs it off, crumples it beyond recognition, and throws it into the car.

Before any other meltdowns occur, I draw a large five-by-five square and hand the first page to my son.

"What are we playing?"

"You'll see."

A moment later, I present the two other papers. "We're going to play Car Bingo—"

"We love Bingo!" cheers Justin.

"It's *Car* Bingo," Emily corrects and points to the twenty-five blank squares. "Um, Mommy, you're missing all the written stuff."

"Yup, but not for long." I take back Justin's blank Bingo card and line it next to the others on the hood of the car. "What things could we see during the drive?" Hesitating, I look around for an idea. "Like a red car." And I write this on each grid in different squares.

"A yellow car!" Justin shouts.

Emily waves her hand like she's answering the winning question to a game show. "I know! A convertible—"

"And a dog. A sports car. Oh, and a motorcycle!" Justin rattles off, getting more energetic with each suggestion.

"Wait a second. If I write any faster, you won't be able to read your Bingo card."

While Justin bites his lip to keep from talking, Emily carefully inspects each grid to make sure that I haven't forgotten anything.

Wow, this is going well. And we're not even at the best part— playing the game.

As soon as I've caught up, they bombard me with more ideas. Ordinary things—a truck, bumper sticker, and billboard sign—to more unusual items—a camper pulling a car, a driver wearing a hat, and the letter *Z*. I dart from paper to paper with Emily overseeing that I'm doing it correctly.

"Hey, kids, we only need one more."

After a short period of silence, Justin starts giggling. "Oh, I have a good one. Someone... picking their nose," he finally says between gulps of air.

At this point, both kids dissolve into laughter and must lean on the car for support.

110

Bite on car	5 people in car	California license plate	Dog	Sports car
Red car	Convertible	Rack on top of car	Bus	Gas Station
Bumper Sticker	Something on the car antenna	✕	Camper pulling a car	Restaurant
Yellow car	Truck	Driver wearing a hat	Police car	Billboard sign
Someone picking their nose	Motorcycle	Construction sign	Bridge	Letter Z

Once the giddiness subsides, I clear my throat to get their attention and announce the last square. "The final item is someone picking their nose."

Again they collapse into fits of giggles while I scribble on the three grids. The game may be set up, but we still have a couple hours of driving, so I swiftly lead them into the car. "Let's get going. Then we can play."

Justin swings open the door, and they scramble inside to fasten their seatbelts. I barely get settled when two hands eagerly reach out for the Bingo grids and pens. "Who wants to be in charge of mine during—"

"Me," Emily predictably says. She takes the last one, writes "Mommy" at the top, and fires off questions. "When should we begin? When the car starts moving? Or when we're on the road, out of the parking lot?"

"On the road," Justin declares in a serious tone since, after all, he's determining the game rules.

Emily nods and motions for me to leave.

I'm about to start the car but shudder at a dreadful thought. *Uh-oh, this game might not last the entire drive. Ugh, then I'll be stuck listening to complaints.*

"Let's play two levels of Car Bingo, so we can play longer," I say. "First, like normal Bingo, you want five in a row. Next, we'll keep playing until someone completes the grid or until we arrive, whichever comes first. Sound good?"

Two pairs of thumbs flash upward.

"Great, and we're off."

We've barely driven when Justin waves his Bingo grid, squealing. "Yellow car and a bumper sticker!"

"Thanks," Emily says, looking around to find these items before crossing off the two squares. "You know, if you announce everything then we'll also see it." Her advice is loud enough to satisfy her big-sister moral responsibility, but not loud enough that he might actually hear her.

Moments later, I catch Emily's attention and whisper, "Bike on car." Oops, too loud because Justin flips his head in all directions.

"A bike? Where? Oh, I see it." He draws a gigantic X and chuckles. "Thanks, Mommy."

Throughout the drive, I hear paper rattling, pens scribbling, and conversations like "How many did you get?" "Where was that?" "Are you close to Bingo?"

The "Are We There Yet?" whines are missing, but definitely not missed.

After a few miles of silence, I hear Justin gasp. "I don't believe it. Pick your nose! Pick your nose!" Not surprising, Emily joins him, and now the back seat sounds like a nose-picking pep rally.

Sure enough, to our left is a man driving with his finger strategically placed near one nostril. With all this excitement, I have to chant along with my giggling pep squad. "Pick your nose! Pick your nose!"

Emily leans closer to Justin for a better view since the guy is on the opposite side of the car. "Look! His finger's inching closer."

"He's almost there!" Justin shouts and presses his face against the window.

This poor oblivious driver. He has no idea that anyone is watching, never mind a fanatic family. Then slowly, his finger creeps over his nostril and slides inside.

"Oh yeah, Car Bingo!" Justin exclaims while the driver sheepishly glances our way and speeds ahead.

19

PASSING TIME WITH THE ALPHABET SEARCH GAME

Keeping Kids Busy and Quiet

"Let's go home already. This is too long. I'm bored," Justin says during our congregation's Saturday morning service.

To his credit, my seven-year-old son starts talking while everyone's reciting a prayer. But it ends before he's finished speaking, so Justin's words echo throughout the now silent sanctuary.

From my other side, Emily groans. "This is boring. I want to leave."

Heads whip around, and I sink in my seat. Some have that disapproving, *keep quiet* frown while other congregants gaze with empathy, probably agreeing with my kids' opinion of this unusually long service.

I glare at my kids and firmly press a finger against my lips. "Shhh!"

Emily scowls and slumps against her chair while my impish son unexpectedly starts grinning.

Uh-oh. What's he up to?

Nervously, I watch as he twitches his nose, scrunches his face, and opens his mouth wide before emitting an explosive, obviously phony, sneeze. "Achoo!"

"God bless you," Emily says at a regular speaking volume and with an all-knowing attitude. Before I can reprimand her for talking, she peers at me and declares, "You can't get mad. That's what you're supposed to say when someone sneezes. *Especially* in a temple."

Justin leans forward and responds, "Thank you," while people nearby glower at us.

By this point, my face is bright lava red from a fifty-fifty mix of embarrassment and anger. Now I'm the one slumping and wishing to disappear. To make matters worse, Emily and Justin start jabbing me on both sides.

Enough!

I want my kids to stop complaining, the congregants to cease staring, and the service to finally end. Turning my wrist ever so slightly, I glance at my watch.

Oh no, at least thirty more minutes!

Near us, I notice other kids tugging at their parents' sleeves, and parents responding with that uncomfortable *please behave* expression. At least I'm not alone, but it doesn't help my situation.

The rabbi asks everyone to stand and read aloud another prayer. I get up and turn to the correct page, but I'm distracted by my thoughts.

We need a game. A quiet one. But what? And where the heck in this passage are people reading? My eyes scan the letters, searching for the written text to match the spoken word.

Letters. Searching. That's it.

I barely catch up when the prayer ends, but now I have a plan. While people noisily sit, I pull my kids into a huddle. "Have you ever played the Alphabet Search game?"

Before they can shake their heads, I keep talking softly. The congregation is singing, so here's my chance to speak without anyone overhearing me.

"Today is your lucky day because we're going to play it." Thrusting a Bible into each of their hands, I briskly ramble off the instructions. "Find all the letters in the alphabet. But it must be the *first* letter of the word, like A in 'Abraham,' B in 'before,' C in 'children,' and so forth. Start with A. Go all the way to Z. Can't skip any letters. Got it?"

Emily's eyes shine.

Justin's face glows, and his thumb starts flipping through the pages.

"Wait. After this song," I say.

Not yet. I have to keep them busy for the rest of this service.

Emily and Justin sit taller, eager for people to finish singing. When the congregation stops, I raise my eyebrows to signal the start of the game.

They nod, grasping their word search board, the Bible.

"Go!" I whisper as quietly as possible.

Justin hunches over, flips open a page and starts sweeping his finger across the lines. Meanwhile, Emily sits motionless except for her hands, which rhythmically turn the pages.

Even though I'm tempted to play, I watch my transformed kids who are attentive and filled with purpose. Okay, maybe not the same as everybody else, but they're quiet and no longer distracting others.

Per the rabbi's request, the congregants rise. That is, everyone except two kids glued to their seats. I gently tap their shoulders. "You need to stand."

"Aw, can we sit and keep searching?" Justin asks, barely looking up.

"Please?" Emily pulls the Bible close to her chest.

"Sure," I whisper, and then sigh with relief before reading the prayer.

Moments later when we sit, an older woman turns around. With a serious face, she motions me closer.

Uh-oh. Now what?

"Your children are behaving nicely. They're quiet and so engaged. Very impressive, reading the Bible at their young age."

Yup, they're occupied all right. Not in the service, but in their Alphabet Search game. And what better source to encourage good behavior than the Bible.

I smile and nod respectfully at her while thinking to myself, *Amen! Hallelujah for peace and quiet.*

Part IV

Yeeks, Everything is Overwhelming

20

WHERE DO YOU LIVE?

Memorizing Things to a Song

My five-year-old daughter's radiant smile abruptly turns into a dumbfounded stare. First, she was excited after we bumped into her friend's mom at the mall and set up a playdate. But now she's speechless.

The mom asks again. "Samantha and I have never been to your house. Where do you live?"

I refrain from answering.

Do my kids even know our address?

Emily glances at Justin who shrugs. "Ask my sister. She's five and knows everything. I'm only three."

There's another awkward moment of silence before Emily tentatively speaks. "Um, we live in San Jose?"

"Yeah, San Jose," Justin repeats, not to be left out.

Wow, they don't know our full address.

Samantha's mom furrows her brow. "But where?"

Now my kids start the fidget dance. They shuffle from one foot to the other and scratch whatever imaginary itch pops up, so I jump in to rescue them. "We live at 5974 Barlington Drive in San Jose, near the movie theaters."

"Fabulous. See you Saturday." She jots down the info and then turns around, disappearing into the crowd.

"Hey, kids, do you know where we live?" I ask, baffled while also feeling guilty that I haven't taught them.

"San Jose! Didn't you hear me?" Emily says.

"San Jose. I said it too!" Justin shouts.

"Yes, but what's our street and house number?"

Blank stares.

Why am I surprised? Unless you live at a simple address, most young kids have a hard time memorizing it. Because it's important to know, I probe further. "What happens if you get lost, and a policeman asks where you live?"

At this point, Emily's eyes widen and Justin steps closer, grabbing her hand.

"Don't worry. You probably won't get lost. But you should know where you live."

Emily glares at me like I asked them to solve a challenging math problem. "Mommy, it's so hard to remember. And we're too little."

"Yeah, I'm only this many," Justin says, sticking out three fingers.

Gee, our address isn't easy. What can I do?

While I try to think of something, I start humming the catchy tune blasting over the mall stereo.

Yes! Learn it with music.

"Hey kids, I'll teach you our address in a fun, and funny, way. But first, I need a song. Any suggestions?" My head darts left and right looking for inspiration. Then I see it: a bunch of boats perched up in a sporting store window. "Here's a song we all know. I'll give you a hint. It's about a boat. A row—"

"Ooh! 'Row, Row, Row Your Boat.' I love that song!" Emily squeals.

"Yes! Yes!" Justin exclaims, joining his sister who is already singing. They march around, lifting their knees and swinging their arms.

"Row, row, row your boat,

Gently down the stream.

Merrily, merrily, merrily, merrily,

Life is but a dream."

When their performance ends, I applaud and lead us to a quiet area of the mall where there aren't any people to hear us.

Yikes! I don't want the entire mall knowing where we live.

"Get ready to learn our address to 'Row, Row, Row Your Boat!'" I start singing the first line of our new song. "I, I, I live at." After repeating this several times, I wave my hands like a conductor to invite my kids, and soon two giggling voices join me.

Next, I introduce the second line. "Instead of 'Gently down the stream,' we'll use our house number." Taking a deep breath, I stretch out the last digit of our address, so it sounds more ridiculous and memorable. "Five, Nine, Se-ven, Fourrrr."

Good thing there aren't more numbers!

Justin flings out his arms while Emily skips around him. They bellow, "Five, Nine, Se-ven, Fourrrrrrrrrrrrrr," accentuating the R until they run out of air.

This next part is tricky, so I clap to keep the beat. I first sing, "Merrily, merrily, merrily, merrily," and then "Bar-ling-ton, Bar-ling-ton, Bar-ling-ton Drive."

Once they get it, we start from the beginning and sing the first three lines. Justin pumps his arms, Emily does a cheerleading routine with pretend pom-poms, and I hop in circles. Luckily, this area of the mall is still empty, so no one is listening.

"And now for the grand finale. We'll change 'Life is but a dream' to the name of our city—"

"San Jose!" they cheer, high fiving each other.

"You got it!" I start clapping to set the beat and sing, "We live in San Jose." We repeat this, making the new words flow with the melody.

"Ready to put it all together?" Surprisingly, it only takes a few times for them to memorize everything.

"Woo-hoo! Congratulations, you both said our address."

"Um, Mommy. We actually *sang* it," Emily says.

"That's okay because you learned it. And now you have a trick for remembering things."

Justin scrunches his face. "Huh? Singing stuff to 'Row, Row, Row Your Boat?'"

"Kind of. The trick is you can use any song to learn something."

"We just have to *sing* it." Emily snickers.

"That's for sure. And now you know where you live, so you don't need to be scared if you ever get lost."

For some reason, Emily starts giggling uncontrollably. She leans over to Justin and whispers in his ear, which also makes him laugh.

"Mommy! Pretend we're lost and you're the policeman," she says, all bubbly.

"Yeah! Ask us where we live," Justin exclaims.

By now, I'm completely confused. *Huh? Happy about being lost?*

"Waah! We're lost, we're lost," they cry through remnants of laughter.

Going along with their plan, I gasp and deepen my voice to take on the persona of a policewoman. "Hi, little girl and little boy. I'm with the police. See, here's my badge," I say, pointing to my imaginary uniform. "I can help you. Where do you live?"

At once, their pretend sobbing stops. With a wide smile, Emily shimmies her hands and steps side to side. She starts singing the first word, encouraging Justin to join her. Holding his head high, he flutters his fingers and sways back and forth. Together they sing their address accompanied with a playful dance.

"I I I live at,

Five, nine, se-ven, fourrrr.

Bar-ling-ton, Bar-ling-ton, Bar-ling-ton Drive.

We live, in San, Jose!"

At the name of their city, they leap in the air, and then take a deep bow.

POSTSCRIPT

Even though it's been over a decade since we moved, my kids and I still know our old address. Whenever we need to remember where we used to live, we instinctively sing the address song— and we can't help but smile.

21

AVOIDING THE MORNING MADNESS

Empowering Kids with a Morning List

As if in a trance, my five-year-old son stares at the white stream of milk flowing off the table, cascading onto the floor and splattering everywhere.

"Uh-oh, the milk spilled," Emily says.

Oh no! We don't have time for this.

I grab a cloth and dart across the kitchen. "Please be more careful. We have to leave for school in eight minutes, and—Yeeks! Why are you both still in jammies? Hurry up!"

Justin stuffs the remaining waffle in his mouth and sprints down the hall.

"It wasn't my fault the milk spilled," Emily mutters as she walks out of the room.

This is crazy. No matter what time my kids wake up, getting out is like a mad dash to the finish line. And this morning's madness is especially ridiculous.

By the time I finish cleaning up, Justin returns dressed, but there's a problem.

"Shorts? I don't think so. It's way too cold outside. Lickety-split, go put on long pants."

"No fair. I run faster in shorts."

"Maybe, but if you get sick, you won't be running at all. Five more minutes!"

Justin disappears, muttering something about needing to be fast because he's the best kindergarten soccer player.

Meanwhile, Emily prances into the room, and thank goodness she's wearing warm clothes. "It's a purple day." She twirls and sweeps her hands across her body to accentuate her purple shirt, purple sweater, and purple socks. "Where are my purple barrettes?"

"I don't know. Choose a different color. We only have four more minutes."

Emily nudges past me and mumbles, "That won't work."

A second later Justin shouts from his bedroom, "I can't find my sneakers."

Really? Another obstacle? The clock keeps ticking.

My adrenaline races as I search under the kitchen table, by the living room couch, and in the front hallway where I discover his missing shoes. Not wasting any time, I create a megaphone with my hands and yell, "Your shoes are by the door. We must leave in ONE minute!"

Emily bolts into the room, now wearing all turquoise. Justin scrambles to the hall and stomps his feet into the sneakers. Frantically, they dash around grabbing their lunches and backpacks, barely avoiding bumping into each other. Finally, we climb into the car and drive to school, but when I pull into the drop-off point, the place is empty like it's a weekend.

"Late again." Emily sighs and opens the door. "We're supposed to be on time."

"Yeah, I'm gonna get in trouble," Justin groans.

They dart down the path while I clench the steering wheel—and my jaw.

Wow, I'm already exhausted. And the day just started.

I have to do something, but right now I need to get to the office and tackle my formidable to-do list.

That's it. We'll create a list to keep us on track at home.

Later that day when we arrive home, my kids do their usual after-school routine. They hang up their coats on the hooks, sit at the kitchen table, and start their homework.

But this time, next to the snacks, there's also a basket of colorful markers. Justin dips a carrot into hummus and watches Emily climb on her chair.

"Ooh! What are we gonna draw?" she asks with delight.

"A morning list for our new racing game. You have to beat the clock and do everything by eight o'clock. And the reward? You get to school on time! Let's make a colorful list with pictures for each item."

"Yeah, because he can't read yet." Emily flashes her big-sister protective smile and sorts through the markers to find her favorite colors.

Meanwhile, Justin continues to munch on carrots, darting his eyes between Emily and me.

I sit at the table with them and point to the basket. "Go ahead, pick a color that has to do with morning."

Shortly, a yellow marker with a glob of hummus appears.

"Yellow won't show up," Emily says, rolling an orange marker across the table. "Use this too."

Before I proceed, I glance at Justin who nods with approval.

Since I don't have the best penmanship, I take a deep breath and write "Morning" in orange and then add a bright multicolor sun. "So, what do you do each morning?"

"Get dressed. We can't go to school naked." Justin giggles.

"Ooh, Mommy, draw a pretty outfit next to it with shoes," Emily squeals.

"Well, we can't have naked kids and bare feet." I write "get

dressed" and draw a purple shirt with polka dots. Underneath, I add "put on shoes" and draw blue shoes with red laces.

Emily waves her hand and blurts out, "I know another one. Brush hair and wear barrettes that match the—"

"Hey!" Justin glares at her. "I don't wear barrettes."

"It's okay, I'll just write 'brush hair.'"

Then Emily flashes a smile to show her sparkling teeth. "We need to brush our teeth and eat breakfast."

My hand quickly moves, writing and drawing each item while I share an idea. "I'll move your breakfast items, so you can easily get them yourself in the morning." Before I can get any push back, I add, "Let's see how fast you can find them tomorrow."

Luckily, my breakfast idea doesn't get any resistance. Justin points to the list and rubs his stomach with his other hand. "We can't forget to add lunch."

While I finish decorating the lunchboxes, Emily giggles. "Oh no, we forgot the most important things!" She jumps up like Tigger and bounces around the table. "Take backpacks and hop in car."

"That's so funny. No homework and no kids." Justin laughs so hard that he falls off his chair.

When we're done, Emily carries our masterpiece to the fridge, avoiding her brother who's still on the floor laughing.

The next morning I wake up my kids and am eager to implement our plan. "Good morning, sunshines! Time to follow our spiffy new list and beat the clock with our racing game."

Even though I'm excited, I'm not sure how smoothly things will go, so I get ready quickly and stride to the kitchen to supervise this morning's activities.

Within moments, Justin runs in. "Oh yeah, waffles!"

So far so good. Long pants and sneakers.

Justin flies by me, opens the freezer, and beams when he sees his beloved breakfast food. Next, he swings open the refrigerator and finds the syrup.

By this time, Emily joins us, gesturing to her purple sweater, purple sneakers, and matching barrettes. She twirls around and announces, "Look, it's a purple day. From head to toe!"

"Nice, your favorite color." I take the list off the fridge and place it on the table. Now it's easier for them to follow.

It's also a gentle reminder not to dawdle.

"Emily, hurry up and eat! Remember, it's a race," Justin exclaims, motioning for her to move faster.

As they eat their breakfast, I glance at the tasks and admire our list. It sure is colorful—

Oops, I forgot to include something.

"Kids, remember to put your dirty dishes in the dishwasher."

There's a brief moment of silence while Emily stops chewing, glances down, and then stares at me with her all-knowing look. "Well, it's *not* on the—"

"It doesn't need to be included because it's part of eating breakfast," I promptly say like I'm a morning list expert, and then immediately change the subject. "So, anything special happening at school today?"

We spend the next few minutes eating, visiting, and cleaning up.

Everything is going well until Justin taps my shoulder. "Um, you forgot something."

Uh-oh. What else did I omit?

"You haven't said how many more minutes until we leave."

Emily chuckles. "*Yelled* is more like it."

Glancing at the clock, I open my mouth, cup my hands like a megaphone, and pretend to shout but instead calmly announce, "Six more minutes."

"Whoa! That's a lot." Justin goes to the fridge and takes out their lunches.

"Yay! We're almost done. We only have to brush teeth, grab backpacks, and hop into the car," Emily says, looking up from the list.

While I wait by the door, I soon hear feet running toward me.

Justin tugs my arm. "Ahem, the time? Did we beat the clock?"

I peek at my watch and pause for dramatic effect.

Emily gasps. "Oh no, are we late? I promised my teacher I'd be on time. Today, I'm the second-grade helper. I'm gonna get in trouble. *Big* trouble. I—"

"Don't worry. You did it! And we're even a little early," I say with a smile.

"Early?" Her mouth and eyes open wider.

Justin pretends to shoot a basket. "Oh yeah, score!"

We each do our celebration dance to the car: Justin bounces, Emily skips, and I hop. Now instead of a tense ride to school, we're calm, cheerful, and energetic.

"What do you think of our morning list?" I ask, pulling into the crowded school driveway.

"The drawings are sooo cute," Emily says.

"I like bouncing to the car." Justin's arms come in and out of the rearview mirror as he waves them wildly.

When it's their turn to get out, I twist around to face my dynamic duo. "Congratulations, you beat the clock in our racing game. And our typical morning madness has turned into a magical morning."

Emily unlatches her seatbelt and reaches over with a hug. "You mean, a *marvelous* magical morning."

22

AVOIDING THE NIGHTTIME NONSENSE

Empowering Kids with a Nighttime List and Fun Incentive

"It's time. Let's go!" I stomp into the living room and stand in front of the TV, not looking forward to another nighttime battle.

"No fair. Not yet!" five-year-old Justin shouts, breaking his TV trance.

Emily springs off the couch and snatches the remote, trying to maintain control of the situation.

Excuse me! Who do they think is boss?

Not waiting another second, I lean over and push the on-off switch. The screen goes dark.

"HEY!" they scream in unison, and I'm not sure whose yell is louder.

"As I was saying, it's time for bed."

Ah, bedtime. One of my least favorite activities with its push-pull arguments. It always ends the same way with nagging and going to bed late.

Justin starts to yawn but clamps his mouth shut. *Too late, I already noticed.*

"See, you *are* tired. Let's go, now!"

"Ju-stin!" Emily glares at her brother who quickly looks away from her intimidating stare. Then her frozen disposition melts as she throws her arms around my waist, covering me with kisses. "Pretty please? Just a little later."

I feel like screaming, but instead, I smirk and redirect my frustration. "Sure, why not stay up *all* night and *never* go to bed. Who cares if you go to school exhausted tomorrow morning."

"Awesome!" Justin looks like he won the world's best prize and leaps off the couch, pumping his fists in the air. "Oh yeah, we get—"

"Hel-lo. She's NOT serious. Humph." Emily grabs her things and saunters out of the room, leaving behind her confused younger brother.

"It's too late for a shower or bath, so brush your teeth and put on jammies," I say. "If you hurry, we'll read more *Harry Potter*."

At the mention of his favorite book, Justin darts down the hall to the bathroom, and I collapse on the couch.

I've got to do something! The morning list worked. Time for a nighttime list. Kids hate going to bed. Hmm, I need an incentive. But what? With each thought, I grip the *Harry Potter* book tighter as I walk down the hall.

"Mommy, it's my turn. Come in here," Justin says, waving me into his room. I snuggle next to him on the bed, and soon Emily dashes in. She looks so cute dressed in her favorite jammies, Angelica from the *Rugrats* TV show—

Yes, that's it. With a triumphant smile and plan for tomorrow, I cuddle close to my two rugrats, and we're swept into the world of *Harry Potter*.

The next day starts extremely well, and once again my kids arrive at school on time.

Thank you, morning list!

After I pick them up, we come home and they do their usual after-school routine. They hang up their coats on the hooks, sit at the kitchen table, and start their homework.

It doesn't take long for Emily to notice the basket with colorful markers. "Yay! Now what are we making?"

Justin shimmies up his chair and grabs the yellow marker in addition to a handful of crackers and cheese.

"You're doing a great job following the morning list, so we're going to create a nighttime one. Woo-hoo! Two days in a row getting to school on time."

Emily cheers while Justin does his best to grin with a mouthful of food.

To focus my team, I roll some markers across the table toward them. The rattling sound immediately brings their attention back to our mission of creating the nighttime list.

"So, how do we get ready for bed?" I ask, writing "Nighttime" at the top.

Emily's arm flies up. "I know!" She points to her face, "wash face" and flashes a smile, "brush teeth."

Justin hands me the green marker, and I write "brush teeth" and draw a toothbrush.

"Nice." Then Emily tosses over the blue marker. "For the toothpaste."

Working fast, I add a swirl on top of the bristles, write "wash face," and include a big happy face.

Justin touches his clothes and smirks.

"Put on jammies and..." With his five-year-old boy humor, he stands up and pretends to pee. "Go... go..." He can barely say the words through his laughter. "Go... pee pee."

Emily shakes her head disapprovingly and gives me the red marker while he climbs back on his chair. Their energy builds as more ideas and markers fly at me, and the paper becomes a colorful list of action items.

This is great. Gee, what else can they do?

Yeah, my kids are young, but they can be more independent. Hesitantly, I announce another task. "Let's add 'make lunch.'"

Everyone stops moving, and two jaws drop.

"You're big enough. I'll even move things in the fridge and reorganize a cabinet, so you can reach items."

After they pout, groan, and reluctantly agree, I write "make lunch" and draw two colorful lunch boxes.

"You'll also choose the next day's clothes. This way you'll get dressed super fast in the morning." Quickly, I include this item before anyone can push back.

"I have another one!" Justin holds out one hand and pinches his nose with the other. "We can't forget to shower—"

"Or take a bath," Emily adds.

My hand sweeps across the page, finishing our nighttime masterpiece with drawings and colors per their art direction.

Now the best part. The incentive!

"Hey, let's make getting ready for bed super fun. If you do everything by seven thirty, we'll meet in the living room and watch our favorite TV show, *Rugrats.*" I glance at my competitive son. "It will be like another race. And we'll start getting ready right after dinner, so you'll have plenty of time." To enlist my head cheerleader, I start chanting, "*Rugrats! Rugrats!*"

Emily instantly squeals, and my pep squad marches around the table, cheering loudly. Waving the list like a flag, I lead us to the fridge where we place it next to the morning one. Then I redirect my team back to the table, so they can start their homework.

Later, after dinner, I remove our nighttime list from the fridge and place it on the table next to my kids. "Let's get ready for bed."

Surprisingly, Emily and Justin cheer, and they race to their rooms. Within minutes, I hear the bathroom faucet turning on and off, closet doors banging, and drawers opening and shutting. It doesn't take long for my kids to skip toward me with clean faces and sparkling teeth.

"You should see what I'm wearing tomorrow," Emily says, hugging me. "Black leggings, my Angelica shirt, polka dot socks, purple sweater, and purple barrettes."

"I'm gonna wear my Sharks shirt and my Sharks sweatshirt and my jeans. I lined it up on the floor. It looks like a headless Sharks fan!" Justin giggles.

"Both outfits sound terrific. Let's make lunch." I bring to the table bread, peanut butter, an assortment of jam, aluminum foil, and a butter knife. "This will be the best lunch ever. Know why? Because you're making it!"

In one smooth motion, Emily takes the foil and tears off a piece, placing it on the table. She hands it to Justin who follows her lead. Next, they become PB&J chefs, creating scrumptious sandwiches oozing with their favorite fillings.

"Yummy," Justin says with a mouthful of peanut butter and jam.

"Mommy, he took a bite!"

"Now I know it tastes good. I don't need to add anything." Justin licks his lips and wraps his delicacy in foil.

Opening the cabinet, I present lunch boxes and bins filled with snacks, easily accessible for anyone under four feet tall. "Chips? Fruit snacks? Don't forget drinks in the fridge. And carrots already in containers."

"Whoa!" Justin digs through the snacks to find his treasure while Emily reaches over and swipes her favorite chips. The three of us glide around the kitchen like a dance routine.

In a little while, Emily holds up the list and reads each item, drawing pretend checkmarks in the air. "We're almost done!"

"What's left?" I ask, biting my lip to not say anything.

"Backpacks by the door, which I'll do. And choose a book for later." She nods at Justin who races out the room and returns waving *Harry Potter*.

Emily turns to Justin and points at one of the remaining items. "It's your turn. What's this?"

He stares at the paper and chuckles. "Water on a stick figure."

"That's right. It's time for my stick figure kids to take a shower or bath," I exclaim, smiling.

"Yay! Then only three more things," Emily says. "Put on jammies, put clothes in the laundry, and go pee."

"Way to go, team. You did it! It's only six thirty. In an hour we get to watch—"

"*Rugrats!*" Justin squeals.

"*Rugrats! Rugrats! Rugrats!*" We cheer, marching to the bathroom, with me cheering the loudest of all.

23

THE CLOTHESPIN SCHOOL FOLDER ORGANIZING GAME

Managing All That School Info

Ugh, Friday afternoon.

I slump against the kitchen counter and wait, breathing deeply to keep my heart from pounding faster. Most people like Fridays, but I dread what's about to—

"Mommy! Look what I brought home." Justin turns over his first-grade end-of-the-week folder and shakes its contents all over the table. I stare speechless as papers pour out like a waterfall.

Then in one smooth movement, Emily grabs and empties her even thicker third-grade packet.

As the piles grow higher, I pull out a chair and sit down with a thump.

Don't get me wrong, I enjoy looking at my kids' hard work, their teachers' comments, and school announcements. But now it's like a tornado hit my normally neat kitchen table. Papers everywhere!

"You need to sign this." Emily slides over a form.

Justin parts his stuff like the Red Sea. Within moments, he withdraws a packet. "Mrs. Smith said I must bring this back on Monday, signed."

"Yay, the yearbook!" Emily squeals. "We need to order and pay."

"Here's Mrs. Smith's newsletter. Surprise! I'm Student of the Week."

"That's wonderful, Justin—"

"Ooh, the third graders are visiting a zoo! You need to sign—"

"And the first graders are going to a farm!"

My head flips back and forth like I'm watching a tennis match. "Okay. What? Where?" I stutter, staring at their field trip forms and other papers shoved at me.

Oh great, I can't even see the table.

Soon their words morph together as I sit heavier in my chair. "Sign... school letter... homework... my painting... form... don't forget..."

It's overwhelming. Now with two Friday folders, school items are multiplying exponentially, and important things are getting buried. At this rate, I'll be drowning each week in paperwork.

Think, Carrie, think. How can I organize this chaos?

For inspiration, my eyes scan the area and notice the refrigerator, stove, laundry room, detergent, iron, clothespins—

Clothespins, yes! My mom used them to organize all kinds of things.

With renewed optimism, I stretch my arms overhead. "Put your hands in the air."

The sound of shuffling paper stops.

Justin tilts his head at Emily who shrugs and releases a permission slip, which floats to the table. Following her lead, he drops his paper and raises his arms.

"Look at this table covered with your impressive work and tons of info. How will I remember what's important and what to do with each item? Wait right here. I have an idea. Oh, you can put your hands down," I say, chuckling. "I just needed you to take a break from going through your folders." Pushing back my chair, I stride to the laundry area, grab a handful of clothespins, and return in a flash.

My mom always said clothespins would come in handy one day. And today is that day!

"These are clothespins." I open my hands and let them fall onto the table. "When your grandparents were young, they didn't have dryers. Instead, they used clothespins to hang their washed clothes on a rope."

With a fixed gaze, Emily asks, "They really didn't have dryers?"

"I know. Weird, huh? Grandma taught me that clothespins could be useful for all kinds of things. So, we're going to use them for an organizing game."

My organizing aficionado clasps her hands while my gaming son pumps his fists.

"Here, try it." The room fills with clicking sounds and giggles as they pinch the clothespins on their hair, shirts, nose, and ears.

"Ouch!" Justin says, clipping it on his nose.

"Earrings!" exclaims my fashionable daughter.

"Very stylish. They're handy little things and can attach to nearly anything. See this mess on the table? Right now, we're losing important papers."

"Like my Student of the Week newsletter." Justin sighs.

"Exactly. In this game, you'll go through your student folder, decide what to do with each item, separate things into piles, and then attach a clothespin. You'll each have a set marked with 'sign,' 'save,' 'recycle,' and a question mark. Then it will be my turn to play, and I'll do what's written on the clothespin."

I grab a basket of markers from the nearby desk, and with a red marker write "sign" on two clothespins. Because Justin is learning to read, I also color the tips red.

"If you want something signed, attach this red 'sign' clothespin. You both mentioned fun field trips. Where are those forms? You certainly don't want to lose these papers. No siree!"

Eagerly, they begin their archaeological dig and soon waggle the permission slips. Promptly, Emily attaches her "sign" clothespin, and Justin follows her lead.

"Terrific, now I know to sign these papers and give them back to you. Next, we need a 'save' clothespin for special things you want to keep. Hey, let's start a nice tradition and review this stack together. What color should we use?"

"Blue," Justin says, handing me the marker. Emily tosses two clothespins and on each, I write "save" and color the tips. Meanwhile, Justin searches for his Student of the Week newsletter. With a big smile, he pinches the blue "save" clothespin to his prized possession.

"Nice! I'm looking forward to reviewing this and other special items with you. Let's create the 'recycle,' one. What color do—"

"Green!" Emily shouts before I have the chance to finish. This time, Justin passes two clothespins, and I quickly write "recycle" and color the ends green.

"Finally, we need a question mark for the huh-I-have-no-idea pile." I take the black marker from my son's waving hand, draw two question marks, color the tips black, and present each child with their own set of clothespins.

"Now can we play?" Justin asks, holding a stack of papers.

"Yeah, let's start," Emily says, pinching a clothespin with each hand.

"Almost, but I'll teach you an organizing trick. First, sort your papers into four areas on the table for 'sign,' 'save,' 'recycle,' and question mark. Then attach the clothespins. It will be much faster this way."

I'm not sure who is more excited to play, the kids or me. Probably me!

"Go, team, go!" I gather papers from my massive stack and distribute them before getting up. "I'll be in the other room if you need help."

Before too long, order appears from the mountain of chaos as Emily and Justin review their art, homework, forms, and miscellaneous items.

A while later, I hear the pitter-patter of feet. "Mommy, come look!" They grab my hand, and we skip toward the kitchen table where I see impressive stacks organized by colored clothespins.

After a family hug, I take the two "save" stacks and lead my kids to the living room. As we snuggle on the couch, they share their work like they won a Nobel Peace Prize.

"Look at my painting!" Justin exclaims, holding up his watercolor landscape.

"Very pretty. I like how you created trees and mountains with long brushstrokes," I say, pointing to the green and blue splotches. His smile widens.

"Look at mine!" Emily presents a colorful pastel painting of a carousel horse covered in glitter.

"Oh, very, *very* pretty!" Justin peers closer to the sparkles.

"Wow, I can feel the horse's excitement twirling around the carousel," I say.

"Can we hang it up?" Emily asks.

"Absolutely. Justin, your masterpiece too?"

He nods and jumps up. "Yeah!"

"But first I have to do something." With a grin, I pinch open the "save" clothespins and attach them to their shirts. "There, it's official. I'm keeping you!"

24

THE ANYTHING-BUT-BORING-MOMMY-DADDY CALENDAR

Making Splitting Time Between Parents Easier for Kids

"Huh? Where do we go when? How do we remember if we're at your house or Daddy's? This is so confusing." Emily blinks away her tears and steps closer to her six-year-old brother who tightly grips her hand.

"I know, it's upsetting," I say, putting my arms around them. "And it's also confusing figuring out where you're supposed to be each day."

"Why can't you and Daddy stay together?" Justin's voice is barely audible, but I understand what he's saying.

So far this conversation isn't going well.

Emily swallows, but her voice cracks. "Where do I keep my Brownie vest for Girl Scouts? Last week I couldn't bring it because I left it at Daddy's house."

I take a deep breath to calm my accelerating heart rate, and try my best to explain. "Your troop meets on Wednesdays. Since you're with me on Tuesday nights, you should always leave it at my house."

Justin stops biting his lip and glances up. "What about my soccer stuff?" If his sister's Girl Scouts vest dilemma had an easy solution, then there's hope for his soccer uniform.

Well, not exactly.

"Your games are every weekend, and each weekend you're with a different parent. Definitely keep your soccer stuff with you, so you'll always have it."

He sighs and droops his shoulders.

They're right. This is very confusing.

With pretend excitement, I try to lighten the mood. "The good news is that you get your wish. Now we're together each afternoon because I can work from home. No more after-school daycare. We'll also be together each night during the week." My fake cheerfulness comes to an abrupt halt. "Um, except Monday nights. Daddy will pick you up after dinner, and you'll spend the night with him."

I ramble on, mistakenly thinking I can clarify the schedule. "Besides Monday, you're also with Daddy every Sunday night. Even when it's a Mommy weekend, you'll go to Daddy's house at five on Sunday."

But my explanation doesn't make things better. Their scowls deepen, and Emily shifts her stance while Justin fidgets.

Ugh, I'm failing miserably. So much for trying to clear things up.

At this point, tears well up in their eyes.

"I know, this stinks. You both need a big hug." I reach out and embrace them tightly. For the next few moments, we cling to each other until I pull myself away, chuckling. "Guess what? Even *I'm* confused with this schedule."

Justin wipes his eyes and giggles. "That's a first. Mommy's confused. Quick, write it down."

Write it down. Of course.

"Hey, that's a great idea. Let's create a schedule and write down where you'll go each day."

"You mean, like a calendar?" Emily says with a smirk.

The snarkiness is back! She must be feeling better.

"Yes, but you're both creative, so let's design a spiffy Mommy-Daddy calendar."

"Ooh, I love making things." Emily darts to the computer and pulls over two more chairs. "Mommy, sit here in the middle."

On my way to the computer, I grab the calendar off the fridge to use as a reference. As I open a new document, my kids lean closer to the monitor. Justin swings his legs and Emily hums a tune. Thank goodness their tears have disappeared. Working fast, I insert a table with seven columns across and several rows down.

"Don't forget the days of the week," Emily says, pointing at the screen.

"And all the numbers," Justin adds.

While I quickly enter all twenty-eight dates for February, my fingers create a rhythm on the keyboard.

"Yeah, now it looks like a calendar. But a *boring* one," Justin says.

"Have no fear, this won't be any boring calendar." I wave my arms like I'm presenting a magic trick. "This is our Anything-But-Boring-Mommy-Daddy calendar."

With a big smile, Justin throws back his arms and belts out, "Our Anything-But-Boring-Mommy-Daddy calendar!" By now Emily is giggling uncontrollably.

"Bravo! Justin, pick a theme for Feb—"

"Hearts!" Emily squeals.

"Hey, Mommy said ME!"

"I'm just helping you. Hearts for Valentine's Day," Emily responds with her protective, big-sister voice.

Justin hesitates. I can tell he doesn't want to give in, but hearts make sense, so he nods.

I open a Google search window, and their enthusiasm soars when an assortment of hearts pops up. Before Emily can choose, Justin jabs his finger at a teddy bear with a pink heart. "This one!"

"Aw, how cute. It looks like the chocolate candies Grandma gave us last year," Emily exclaims.

Instantly, I copy and paste two images on each side of the month's name.

"Let's add it to the fourteenth," Emily exclaims, making elaborate gestures in front of the screen.

Bam, the heart teddy bear now also adorns the Valentine's Day square.

"Nice. Let's decorate the entire calendar. Justin, you go first. What do you want, and where should I put it?"

He thinks for a moment and then roars, curling his fingers like claws. "A tiger." Within seconds, Google shows an assortment of these exquisite animals.

"This one! And here," he says.

Done. Our calendar now has a tiger.

"And a lizard," he adds, sneaking in another suggestion.

Emily glares at her brother with the you-don't-think-I'm-paying-attention-but-I-am look. "Then it's MY turn."

Keeping up with their requests, I copy and paste items into assigned areas until a colorful calendar appears. We have all kinds of animals: a kitten, puppy dog, dolphin, fox, hummingbird, flamingo, elephant, and even a shark. There are also festive items: a present surrounded by confetti (Emily's choice), a layered cake

(Justin's idea), and an open box of chocolates (my contribution). Since February is first-grade science month, we include a bright planet at the bottom of the page.

When I'm done, Emily applauds our work. "It's so pretty."

Justin nods. "This was so much fun to—"

"Can we do one for March, April—"

"Can Daddy get a copy?"

"Yes, yes, yes, and yes," I say, carefully responding to each of their rapid-fire remarks and questions. "Also, there's something extra special this month. February vacation! Let's add 'no school' to our spiffy calendar."

As they cheer loudly, my heart pounds.

But this time from excitement. Yay! My kids are no longer upset and things are going well. With all this positive, exuberant energy, my confidence level is soaring and—

Then Emily gasps.

Uh-oh.

Thankfully, her sharp inhalation turns into giggles.

"Wait! We forgot something super important," she says.

My head flips from Emily, to the monitor, to Justin, and then back to Emily.

What's wrong?

Our calendar has the days of the week, dates, and even pretty images.

"It's so funny! We forgot to include when we're with you and Daddy."

Justin shakes his head. "That was the whole point."

"Now it's our Anything-But-Boring-Calendar *without* the Mommy and Daddy." Emily laughs.

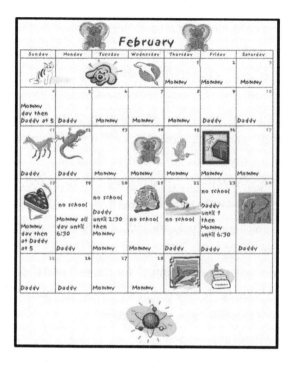

Oops, so much for clarifying the parenting schedule.

"You're right." I return my fingers to the keyboard and ask, "What do you remember from the world's most complicated schedule?"

Justin throws his arms around me. "Mommy every day after school!"

"You betcha." I kiss the top of his head and start typing.

Emily slowly raises her hand. "Something about Daddy and Mondays."

"Correct. On Mondays, Daddy picks you up after dinner." I type "Daddy" at the bottom of each Monday square, and while I'm at it, add "Mommy" for the other weeknights. "You're with me on Tuesday, Wednesday, and Thursday nights."

"I think I know one. It has to do with soccer." Justin pauses as he furrows his brow. "Oh yeah, I remember. Always carry my stuff because you take turns on weekends."

"Very good. Now, let's fill in Saturdays and Sundays as either a Mommy or Daddy weekend." My hand remains still, holding the mouse, and I can't help smiling. Sure, partly from the upbeat mood, but mostly because of a stark realization.

"Hey, kids, how funny. Now I'm the one confused. Who were you with last weekend? Was it Daddy?"

"Yup." Snickering, Emily adds, "Looks like *you* need a copy of our calendar."

"No kidding." I type "Mommy" for the first and third weekend nights, and "Daddy" for the remaining ones. Additionally, I include the schedule for their February vacation.

"Hey, where are we tonight?" Justin asks. Before I have a chance to respond, he giggles. "Never mind, I'll just look at our Anything-But-Boring-Mommy-Daddy calendar."

"Me too," Emily exclaims.

"Me three! I better print lots *and lots* of copies!"

25

THE SPIFFY PROJECT PLANNING CALENDAR

Avoiding Procrastination

Thunk! How can my kids' backpacks be that heavy? And today the bags sound especially loud hitting the floor.

Goodness! They're only in first and third grade, so they shouldn't have that much homework. At this rate, Justin and Emily will need a wheelbarrow in high school to carry all their stuff.

"Yay! My first book report." Emily waves *Charlotte's Web* and prances around the kitchen table, jumping so high that her ponytail sways with each step.

Sitting quietly, Justin observes his older sister. He stuffs handfuls of snacks into his mouth, eating as much as possible before she sits down.

"Very exciting," I say, watching my girl twirl and skip. "When's it due?"

"Around Thanksgiving." She collapses on her chair and snatches whatever is left of the cheese and crackers. "I have lots of time."

My body tenses. "Um, not really. November is only two weeks away."

Oh no, my daughter is already showing signs of procrastination. What happens when she's older and juggling multiple assignments?

"Mommy, don't worry. I'll start reading later." Emily sighs and takes out packets of other homework.

I will not micromanage, I will not micromanage becomes my mantra, and I distract myself by opening my work laptop.

The next day after school while my kids eat snacks and tackle their homework, I make myself wait five whole minutes before starting the anti-procrastination inquisition.

"So, how's *Charlotte's Web?*"

"I don't know," Emily mumbles, focusing on her math worksheet.

Sensing that his big sister may get in trouble, Justin looks up with a grin, awaiting my response.

I swallow, blink a few times, open my mouth, and then dart out of the room to start a load of wash. *Do not tell her what to do. Do not tell her what to do.*

For the rest of the week, the scene repeats, and I refrain from saying anything.

The following Tuesday, Emily neatly lays out her homework, except for one thing: the book.

Unbelievable! She hasn't even started.

"How's the pig in *Charlotte's Web?*" I ask, biting my lip to keep from ranting and raving.

"I still don't know. I'll read it another day. This stuff is due now. That's due around Thanksgiving, in November."

Justin smirks. "Uh, next week is the Halloween parade. Then it's November."

"Emily, he's right. It will be here before you know it."

Life is stressful enough without procrastinating big projects. But what can I do? At work, we have zero tolerance for missing deadlines, and our team completes tasks because we do project planning.

Planning, that's it. Why can't we do this at home? We can. And we will. Starting now!

Not wasting any more time, I dart to the computer and open a document. My fingers tap on the keyboard as I insert a table, create a grid, and type the days of the week. I add "Project" and "Due Date" at the top, print a copy, and grab this soon-to-be spiffy project planning calendar out of the printer.

"Whatcha doing?" Justin asks, licking his lips to savor every last bit of hummus.

"We're going to create a project planning calendar. It's like playing a game with goals, rules, and challenges." I glance at Emily who continues to pout. "This is the first step for any project."

"Ooh, like my book report?" Her defensiveness dissolves into a glowing smile.

"Yes, exactly. When something is due in a month, it's easy to think, 'Oh, I'll just do it later. I have *plenty* of time.' When you plan, you stay on top of a project. You avoid last-minute rushing. And you meet the deadline, which is the goal."

I pause to catch my breath. There's a week's worth of pent-up thoughts!

"Planning is used for lots of things. Remember when our friends drove cross-country to Walt Disney World?"

"Yeah, they had a big map with pins on it," Emily says.

"They went to lots of places," Justin adds.

"That's correct. They figured out in advance where to stop along the way. This planning helped them get to Walt Disney

World on time." I slide three chairs next to each other, wave the paper, and motion my kids to the kitchen table. "Your project planning calendar is your roadmap. It will help you finish the book report by the deadline and without rushing."

"Um, Mommy, the paper's blank," Justin says.

"Not for long. Emily, when's the exact due date?"

She pulls out her assignment while I grab our calendar from the fridge. "November twenty-seventh," she announces in her most grown-up, I-got-this voice.

"Here's a pencil," I say, handing it to Emily.

So exciting! I get to teach my kids project planning.

"Write the project name, like '*Charlotte's Web* Book Report' and the due date." I slide over the book so she can copy the title.

Emily props herself up and grips the pencil like a valuable treasure.

Justin watches, barely moving, and then exhales when she finishes.

"Look! I added a happy face." Her smile is as wide as the one she drew.

"I like it," Justin exclaims, applauding.

"You're off to a great start. Now you need to turn this into a project planning calendar. We'll use our fridge calendar as our guide. Start with today, Tuesday, October twenty-fourth, and write the dates through November twenty-seventh when it's due. Write the numbers—"

"I know! I know what to do." Emily grasps the pencil, and the blank grid is transformed.

"Beautiful. Think about traveling. When we drive somewhere, we determine our arrival time by knowing the number of miles. It's similar for book reports. Knowing the number of pages and chapters helps us understand the scope of this project. How many pages are in *Charlotte's Web?"*

Emily flips to the end of her book. "One hundred ninety-two."

"And chapters?" I ask, turning to the table of contents so she can easily find the info.

"Twenty-two."

"This is important, so you'll want to include it."

Justin taps the bottom of the page, I spell the words, and Emily writes.

"Next, what's the assignment? What do you need to do?"

She takes out the packet, and her face lights up. "Read the book. Answer questions. Yay, draw a picture!"

"How fun. You love reading and drawing. Let's turn this into your spiffy project planning calendar and plan what you'll do each day. Otherwise, can you imagine if you didn't start until *right* before the due date?"

Emily gulps and Justin plops his head in his hands.

I wince and shake my head. "Nope, we don't want that."

We certainly do not!

Phew, they're onboard the procrastination avoidance train. I'll probably have to explain this again when Justin gets older, but onward for Emily.

"Woo-hoo, let's start planning! The due date is super important, so you want this to stand out. Circle the number twenty-seven and write 'Due Date.' If you want, you can even underline the words."

As I spell out the info, Emily takes a deep breath and carefully completes this square.

"Wonderful. Want to learn one of my super-duper planning tricks?"

Project:	Charlotte's Web Book Report ☺					
Due Date:	Nov 27					
Sunday	**Monday**	**Tuesday**	**Wednesday**	**Thursday**	**Friday**	**Saturday**
		Oct 24	25 Read 1+2	26 Read 3+4	27	28
29	30 Read 5+6	31	Nov 1 Read 7+8	2 Read 9+10	3 Read 11+12	4
5	Read 6 13+14	Read 7 15+16	Read 8 17+18	Read 9 19+20	Read 10 21+22	11
12	13 Report	14 Report	15 Report	16 Report	17 Report	18
19	20 Finish! ☺	21	22	23 Thanks-giving	24	25
26	Due Date ☺					

192 pages   22 chapters

Both kids nod, especially Justin who loves a competitive advantage.

"Even though November twenty-seventh is the *real* deadline, you should plan to finish a few days or even a week earlier. What happens if you get sick and can't work on your book report? If you build extra time into your schedule, you can still finish by the deadline." I plop my finger on the twentieth. "Let's allow a week buffer. Write 'Finish' here."

Emily spells aloud while writing each letter. "F-I-N-I-S-H." Then she adds an exclamation mark and another happy face. "Look! I'll be glad when I'm done."

"That's so cute. Since weekends are jam-packed with activities, let's leave weekends off this planning calendar. If you end up working on your book report, great, you'll be ahead of schedule. You can use weekends to catch up if you fall behind. Go ahead and cross off Saturdays and Sundays before the finish date."

I wait for Emily to finish drawing an X on these days and then continue explaining.

"What other days have something going on?" For a clue, I point to the pumpkins on our counter.

"Halloween!" Justin exclaims.

"That's for sure. Put a big X on this date. I doubt you'll have time to work on your report."

Gripping the pencil, Emily draws an X on October 31 and then sketches a jack-o'-lantern. She looks up. "What about Alexandra's party?"

"Yes, that's the Friday before." I point to the twenty-seventh where Emily nudges my finger away so she can draw another X.

"Oh, don't forget the World Series!" Justin shouts.

Emily rolls her eyes. "No, that's for *your* spiffy project planning calendar. I don't care about baseball."

"It's helpful to understand that your project has two parts," I say, getting us back on track. "First, you read. Second, you do the report by answering questions and—"

"Drawing a picture!" Emily cheers.

"Yes, that's right. To plan, we work backward from the finish date, November twentieth. How many days do you want for the report part? Three days? Four? Five—"

"Oh, pick five! I used to be five," my six-year-old son says, grinning.

"You're so cute. Okay, five days," Emily says and then whispers in my ear, "This seems like enough time."

"Five sounds great. Good thing Justin isn't one." I chuckle while Emily taps her pencil to keep me focused. "This is the final part of the project, so count five days from the finish date—"

"I got it. Just tell me what to write on the five squares."

"How about 'Report?'"

With a quick nod, she writes "Report" across the row and then jumps up waving her sheet. "Look, it's filling up. Hip, hip, hooray! My spiffy project planning calendar. Hip, hip, hooray!"

Since the next part is complicated, I wait for her to settle down before continuing. "Now we can add the first part of your project, reading the book. We'll use math to figure out how many chapters you'll need to read each day. Take the number of chapters and divide by the number of days left on your calendar. That's twenty-two chapters divided by twelve days."

After a blank stare, I give the answer. "This is tricky. It's about two. To stay on schedule, you should read two chapters each day."

"Only two? Easy, I can do that."

"Woo-hoo! That means we did a good job planning," I say. After a round of high fives, I give the final set of instructions. "Start at the last blank square, November tenth. Write 'Read' and include the final two chapters, twenty-one and twenty-two."

For the next few minutes, I dictate which two chapters Emily needs to read each day, and she writes these chapter numbers underneath "Read." When she gets to today's date, she looks up. "Hey, what about today? It's empty?"

"According to this plan, you can start tomorrow. You can always do more and be ahead of schedule. You just don't want to fall behind."

"Hooray!" She twirls around, holding the paper high. "My spiffy project planning calendar is done. Dooooooone!"

"There's one more thing," I say.

"Huh? What else?" Emily stops moving and furrows her brow.

"You'll like this part. Whenever you finish a task, you'll draw a big check mark on that item. This way you'll know how you're doing and where you are with the project."

Justin jumps up, pumps his arms, and cheers, "Em-i-ly! Em-i-ly" while she dances around the table.

"Congrats, sweetie." After we spend a few minutes celebrating, I lower my voice to a whisper. "Ready for the best part?"

The room becomes silent.

"If you start today, you'll be ahead of the game."

"Yay, I love reading!" Emily grabs the book and skips to her room chanting, "*Charlotte's Web! Charlotte's Web!*"

After she leaves, I sit down, sigh deeply, and turn to Justin. "Phew, no more procrastination."

"What's that?" he asks.

"It's postponing and avoiding a task you need to accomplish."

"Huh?"

With a smile, I chuckle and swoop him into a big hug. "Don't worry about it. That's the beauty of a spiffy project planning calendar. There's no such thing as procrastination!"

Part V

Oh Yeah, Live Life to the Fullest

26

A VERY IMPORTANT APPOINTMENT

Taking Time to Cherish Life

This morning while driving to school, my eight-year-old daughter squeals loudly from the backseat, "I'm so excited!"

Who can blame her. My kids and I have eagerly awaited this day, and hooray, it's finally here.

Justin launches into a silly dance, swinging his arms and legs wildly with the seatbelt tugging as he moves. "Hip, hip hooray! Yay, it's today!"

"That's right. This afternoon we have a very important appointment." Through my enthusiasm, I can't help sighing. If only I can stifle that nagging inner voice. *You shouldn't take them out of school early. You shouldn't take them out of school early.*

Sitting more confidently, I try and squash my guilty conscience. Big deal if my kids leave a little earlier. Besides, today we're starting a tradition that we'll continue and cherish for years.

"I'll pick you up one hour earlier. Please be ready. We cannot be late." Pausing, I look in the rearview mirror to lock eyes with both kids. "That's one thirty, sharp."

Justin's energy morphs into a karate gesture, his hands and feet flying. "Hi-ya! One thirty, sharp."

"Not a minute after," Emily says with her best mommy imitation.

When we arrive, I turn into the school's driveway. "Don't worry. I'll let the office know you'll be leaving early for—"

"A very important appointment," they say, giggling.

The car inches forward and stops at the drop-off point. I turn around with a smile and initiate our new going-to-school tradition. "See you later, alligator."

"In a while, crocodile," Emily says.

They unbuckle their seatbelts, open the door, and slide out of the car.

"See you soon, racoon." Justin swings the door shut.

"Time to go, buffalo." Then my serious side regains control and pushes aside all playfulness. I quickly lower my window. "What time will I get you?"

Justin "humphs" and glances at Emily who is already shaking her head. In sync, they reply, "One thirty!" and skip down the path to their respective classrooms.

Before leaving for work, I pull into a parking spot to go inside the office.

Wait. Seriously? I'm telling the school staff in person?

I'm the world's worst liar. One look at my face and they'll know something's up.

Instead, I grab my phone to avoid a guilty face-to-face interaction.

The secretary answers on the first ring. "Dwight Elementary."

"Hi, Alice. It's Carrie, Emily and Justin's mom."

"Hi, Carrie. Can you believe it's Friday?"

"Time sure flies." I take a deep breath to suppress my pounding nerves. "Um, I'm calling because Emily and Justin have a very important appointment. So, um, I have to pick them up early."

Yeeks, my voice is getting squeakier. A sure telltale sign that I'm up to something.

"That's fine, what time?"

I cough to regain my normal speaking voice. "One thirty."

"Okay, see you then. Have a great day."

There, that wasn't bad. Or did she suspect something? Whatever. I push away any doubts and drive to work.

Thank goodness, the day flies by faster than usual. Later, when I gather everything to leave the office, my team snickers. "Enjoy your very important appointment," they say, accentuated with finger quotation marks.

Because there isn't any traffic, the drive is easy, and now my lingering guilt has transformed into eager anticipation. I hop out of the car and run into the school office to find Emily and Justin. As expected, my euphoric kids are waiting, squirming in their seats.

"Mommy's here!" Emily immediately leaps off her chair.

"Yay!" Justin darts across the room and gives me a tight hug.

"Let's skedaddle." I hold open the door and smile at the secretary, who thankfully is still on the phone.

Emily and Justin bolt outside, sprinting to the car. We toss backpacks in the trunk and scramble into the car. When I hear the clicks of two seatbelts, we're off, and before too long, zipping along the freeway.

"My friends are so jealous," Emily says.

"Yeah, my friends kept saying 'No way!'" Justin boasts.

Then their conversation digresses into nonstop dialogue with a mixture of giddy laughter and delightful squeals. Finally, we arrive at our exit.

"I'm so happy, I could burst," Emily says, dancing in her seat.

"Go, Mommy, go!" Justin pumps his fists energetically as if he can make the car accelerate.

We swerve along the road and turn into a parking lot. Yeeks! A very crowded parking lot.

"Oh no! So many cars." Emily's exhilaration plummets.

Did she think we'd be the only ones here?

"Sweetie, everyone's been waiting three years for—"

"Hurry up and find a spot. We can't miss any of it," Justin shouts.

"Park farther away. We'll walk!" Emily is a bit too pushy, but it is excellent advice.

I grasp the wheel, and as predicted, there's an empty spot toward the back, so I zoom in. Right when I stop the car, my kids unlatch their seatbelts and leap out.

"Come on!" Justin grabs our hands and drags us, running through the maze of cars. "We're almost there."

As we get closer, Emily sighs. "Oh no! Look at all these people."

Sure enough, a long, crowded line wraps around the building.

"Keep going!" Justin yanks us to run faster.

"Wait," I say, catching my breath. I drop his hand, reach in my purse, and pull out three tickets. "We don't need to stand in line. Look what I have!"

"Mommyyyy!" They howl and start their we're-so-excited dance.

Wow, this is better than expected. It's like I presented the last three Willy Wonka Golden Tickets.

After my kids stop hooting and hollering, Justin exclaims, "Let's go!"

Even though we don't need to rush, we still forge ahead to the entrance. When we arrive, I swing open the door, and they dash inside, ducking under my arm.

Oh my, sensory overload with shining bright lights, pungent popcorn, and loud exhilarated voices.

"Yay! We're here on opening day," Justin says.

"It doesn't get better than this." Emily clasps her hands.

Amidst the cacophony of sounds, I hear my name. "Carrie! Over here." Immersed in the crowd is my friend Lisa, energetically waving while her three kids hop like bunnies.

"We'll be right there," I yell, leading my kids, and soon I fly into Lisa's open arms. Now *five* kids are bouncing up and down.

"So, you also picked up your kids early from school for a *very* important appointment," I whisper in her ear.

"Ah, yes! They have a doctor's appointment." Then with a wink, she adds, "With Dr. Potter, of course."

We hold hands and hustle into the bustling movie theater. Hooray! The first Harry Potter film: *Harry Potter and the Sorcerer's Stone.*

Thanks for reading! Turn the page to download free extras.

FREE BONUS MATERIALS

Don't miss out on downloading these useful tools at bit.ly/ParentingExtras

- The images that accompany this book, which show the charts, calendars, and tools that Carrie created.

- A project planning calendar template to help teach your child how to manage and stay on top of projects.

- Step-by-step directions on how to complete a project planning calendar. This can be tricky, so this one-page document explains what to do.

- A Car Bingo template and cards for entertainment during your next long road trip.

DISCUSSION QUESTIONS

There are many ways to deal with everyday challenges using playful, positive parenting. So we can inspire and learn from each other, I encourage you to start a conversation. Here are some issues to discuss with book clubs, reading groups, family, and friends.

1. What are your favorite takeaways from the book?

2. Which are your favorite stories? What do you like about them?

3. Choose a story and discuss how Carrie overcomes that challenge. If you've been in a similar circumstance, what have you done? What are other ways to handle this situation?

4. How do you cope with frustrating parental moments?

5. Games can be very effective. Have you created or used games to get children to do something? What have you done? Did these stories spark any new ideas?

6. Children can easily get restless, especially when you want them to sit quietly. When have you experienced this problem? What are your tips and tricks for making waiting more tolerable?

7. No one likes being scared, and fear can be impairing. Have you used nontraditional ways to conquer phobias? What did you like about Carrie's approaches? Select a common fear and discuss some coping techniques.

8. Stress management is important, even at an early age. Carrie uses imaginary bubbles to teach mindful breathing. Have you used other techniques to teach children stress coping skills? What happened and what do you recommend?

9. How did this book change your perspective on parenting? How can you be a more positive and playful parent? Which of Carrie's techniques do you want to try?

10. Having a playful, positive attitude is effective not just for parenting. How can you adapt these strategies to your adult life?

11. Do you remember any playful parenting experiences from your childhood?

ACKNOWLEDGMENTS

Writing this book was rewarding, but I couldn't have done it alone. I want to thank all the people who graciously offered their help in various ways.

I give heartfelt thanks to Andrew, my boyfriend and life partner, who has been incredibly enthusiastic and supportive from the very beginning of this monumental project. He has eagerly been by my side as the first and last person to read each chapter numerous times. His endless love, strategic direction, copy editing expertise, content suggestions, and clever wit not only improved the book but also helped make it a reality.

I'm deeply appreciative of my children who make parenting better than I could ever have imagined. Without them, this book wouldn't exist, and it's been fun reminiscing about their childhood to spark story ideas. Many thanks to my daughter for spending hours reviewing and editing chapters, brainstorming marketing ideas, and cheering me on with her "You got this!" enthusiasm. A big thanks to my son who kept me centered when I felt overwhelmed, simplified the reviewing process, and listened intently when I responded to his question, "So, how's the book?"

Thank you, Alex, for reading each chapter several times and providing wonderful feedback. She was always available, happy to help, and got back to me quickly. I am grateful for Debby who gave constant support throughout the entire process, and for applying her speech and language expertise to make sure each story properly reflected the children's ages. Thanks to Peri, whose coaching, suggestions, and mentoring improved my writing and kept my spirits high. Thank you, Alice, for reading, sharing clever ideas, and providing nonstop encouragement. Carrie's comments and love for my book were like shots of adrenaline and greatly appreciated. Much gratitude to Garima who provided insightful feedback on many chapters, brainstormed marketing ideas, and was a marvelous Millennial social media coach. Thank you, Ginny and Monica, who were amazing cheerleaders, keeping my confidence high when I questioned what the heck I was doing writing a book.

During various stages of the writing process, I reached out to the following people who helped make a difference. I am very thankful for their time, comments, and honesty, which kept raising the bar. Thank you, thank you, thank you Alexa, Barbara, Cari, Chad, Dionicia, Dwayne, Elissa, Jeff, Jill, Jody, Joy, Kiri, Marta, Mary Ann, Maxine, and Reina.

I can't forget two other influential people who jump-started this book. Thank you Dr. Nguyen who for many years was intrigued by my playful parenting approach and kept wanting to hear more stories. At the end of each annual physical exam, she always said, "You should write a book!" Then, years later at a Mount Holyoke College event, I met alumna and author Karen. She not only excited me about making my dream a reality, but she also suggested the format of quick-to-read stories for busy parents.

Last, but certainly not least, I thank my parents for being terrific role models. Even though they're no longer here, they are with me every day, cheering me on.

ABOUT THE AUTHOR

Karen Thurm Safran works as a marketing executive in K-12 education technology, making learning fun for kids. She has a BA degree in psychology from Mount Holyoke College and an MBA from Santa Clara University. Even though she works in an exciting industry, being a mom is by far her favorite job. As a parent, she gets to apply her problem-solving, organizational, and leadership skills to empower those she loves most—her two children.

When Karen's children were young, she found that parenting became more enjoyable, rewarding, and empowering when she used a positive and playful style, innovatively creating games to deal with everyday challenges. She wrote *Parenting—Let's Make a Game of It* in memory of her parents, and to spark playful parenting, encourage out-of-the-box thinking, and ease frustrating moments.

Connect with Karen at the following places:
Website: www.ParentingLetsMakeAGameOfIt.com
Instagram: www.instagram.com/Karen.Thurm.Safran.Author
Facebook: www.facebook.com/AuthorKarenThurmSafran
Pinterest: www.pinterest.com/ParentingLetsMakeAGameOfIt
Email: Karen@ThurmSafran.com

PLEASE POST A REVIEW

Thank you for reading this book. I would greatly appreciate if you could take a few minutes to post a review on Amazon. Your feedback is important and will help other readers. Visit Amazon, search for the book, click on the "Customers Reviews" link, and select the "Write a Customer Review" button. Thanks!